A FAMILY AFFAIR...

Camping can spell great fun for the whole family—particularly when the outdoor chef follows the helpful hints of Bill Riviere, former Maine guide and author of the *Campers' Bible*.

In his new book Mr. Riviere offers a step-by-step guide to outdoor cooking, from building the fire to preparing dessert—from selecting the right food and equipment to making vacation meals tastier and more manageable.

Plus lots more . . . hundreds of the author's unusual and delicious recipes from campsites all over America—even including some from the Ontario Indians, Dakota cowhands, and Texas *chicanos*.

Truly, a must for all forest-bound families!

Family Campers' Cookbook

Bill Riviere

Originally published in hard cover by
Holt, Rinehart and Winston

A Tower Book

To *my* family campers—
Eleanor,
Bill,
and Jo-Anne.

Preface

IN WRITING the Family Campers' Cookbook, I've tried to keep in mind that camp cooking should result not only in good eating but also in pleasure for the outdoor chef. A man should enjoy his work; he should delight in his hobby. Camp cooking may well be both. Because the cook, too, needs time for lazing in the sun, I've dealt primarily with simple, uncomplicated techniques and recipes. You'll find no exotic Trout Amandine or he-mannish Braised Moose Hocks described or even suggested. I've made some exceptions, however. Bean-hole beans, for example, and a New England clambake are not insignificant projects, but such cooking has been included only for those who derive pleasure from rattling pots, pans, and kettles.

Thanks are due Dick and Janice Williams of Newbury, Massachusetts. Dick publishes the bi-monthly *Campfire Chatter* for the 12,000 families of the New England Family Campers Association, while Janice writes a cooking column for the magazine. Both graciously consented to my including many recipes submitted by members for her column. Where else can one get better family camping recipes than from family campers?

I owe thanks, too, to dozens of north-woods guides, woodsmen, lumber-camp cooks, some of whose names I've long forgotten but whose graciousness in sharing cooking hints I well remember. My son, Bill, took time out from engineering studies to draw the diagram of the camp kitchen in Chapter V. My daughter Jo-Anne's contribution was indirect but nonetheless notable. She was patient and understanding in the face of a not-always-cordial disposition I'm reported to develop when I'm birthing a book. To my wife, Eleanor, goes special appreciation. She brought midnight coffee, proofread the manuscript, researched facts which I always seemed to need in a hurry, and helped me fuss no end with cooking gear and grub for photographs.

—B. R.

Contents

Chapter I

Planning
and
Setting Up

THERE'S AN old woodsman's adage that a wood pile warms you twice—"once in the cuttin' an' ag'in in the burnin'." By the same token, a family camping trip can be enjoyed twofold—first in the planning and again when the actual adventure unfolds.

With the living room knee-deep in catalogs, road maps, and campground guides, you'll hardly notice the wintry gale howling outside as each member of the family conjures up blue skies, a chuck box bulging with devil-may-care calories, a camp stove that functions as well as the advertising claimed it would, a snug tent or trailer by a corn meal-colored beach, and congenial camping neighbors who marvel at the professional skill with which you set up your outfit. Fireside dreams are like that.

Add a pinch of practical planning, however, and the joys of the actual trip may well match those of the dream. Planning won't hold off a three-day rain, of course, or guarantee neighbors who enjoy late-evening coffee, but it will assure that the cook's favorite pot won't be left behind; vitally important to those who know that a camp chef without his pet tools is often difficult—yea, verily—impossible to live with!

Granted, there's more to trip planning than making sure a skillet isn't overlooked. There's the matter of learning something about the camping area; possibly a tentsite to be reserved; the choice of an interesting route; repairing a leaky tent or attaching a new sleeping bag zipper. However, since innumerable suggestions are to be found in general camping literature, overall trip planning won't be discussed here. Our concern is primarily with the camp cook's problems.

Camp cooks hold two viewpoints regarding the demand for their services. One school—and this one includes the vast majority of campers—maintains that getting camp meals is incidental to other outdoor fun. Campers—no different from golfers or mah-jong players, so someone prepares three meals each day. To some extent I throw my lot in with this thinking in that I'm convinced that no camp meal should take more than an hour to prepare. If we must eat three times daily, well and good, but let's not keep the camp chef chained to the camp stove while other members of the family are fishing, boating, swimming, or hiking. Menus, generally, should be simple with a marked absence of exotic dishes that require lengthy preparation, but this need not imply dull, unimaginative, and monotonous meals. On the contrary, while the chef must not be a slave to assorted appetites, he should be careful not to fall into a "come-and-get-it-or-I'll-throw-it-away" attitude, without pride in his productions.

The second viewpoint is that of the camp cook who *enjoys* long hours over his pots and grills. Some years ago, in Wisconsin's Chequamegon National Forest, I once devoted a full week to open fire cooking while my family enjoyed the more conventional camping fun. I'd acquired a new assortment of reflector and Dutch ovens in which I concocted every camp dish I'd ever heard about, short of leg o' lamb. We had food to burn and, in fact, during experiments some of it did! The prime purpose of this trip, as far as I was concerned, was outdoor cooking.

The Maine Guides (in Maine, "Guide" is capitalized) of the Pink Tree State's Rangeley Lakes region are as handy about a cook fire as they are with a fly rod or an outboard motor. For years, guides from other sections of the state have scorned the Rangeley men for "inventing the nine-course cook-out." Their fame spread and eventually forced *all* guides to spend more time cooking when they would rather have been fishing. However, there was method in this Rangeley madness. As it will in any good fishing waters, angling action sometimes slumped into the doldrums. Sportsmen became restless and even questioned their guides' skill. It was then that the Rangeley Guides took their clients ashore for a noonday luncheon that often consisted of broiled steaks, deep-fried onion rings, French-fried potatoes, tossed salad, coffee that would float a hatchet, and like as not, chocolate cake or gingerbread with whipped cream. One guide, whose sole acquaintance with French cooking occurred in the French-Canadian lumber camps, repeatedly astounded his Park Avenue guests with crêpes suzette! This sort of a meal, eaten on the shores of a spruce-fringed wilderness lake, made a memorable day even if the biggest fish was hardly worth bragging about.

These two widely separated approaches to camp cooking form the options open to family campers. Meals may be kept basically simple so that the cook, too, can enjoy other outdoor sports, or if the chef considers campfire cooking a sport in itself, meals may be as elaborate as his imagination and skill permit. Fortunate are the campers whose numbers include a dedicated camp chef!

Whether meals are incidental or an end in themselves, a camp cook's basic tool is a check list on which is noted *every* item necessary for or contributing to camp meals, from asparagus to zwieback. My own list is several years old and it was started during the winter, months before our first camping trip got under way, so that I could add items as I was reminded of them or as I acquired them. It's nigh on to impossible to compile a complete list at one sitting unless you have a master list as a guide. To that end, I've included my list in the Appendix.

No item, no matter how obvious, should be omitted from the list. Who'd forget the can opener? I did once so that we opened cans with an axe during an eight-day canoe trip and my left thumb still bears the scar of an encounter with a can of cream-style corn!

Between trips, or during the off-season, a camp cook's equipment is often borrowed for household use, hence the need for careful checking. My wife, for example, appropriates my cast-iron square skillets during the winter, but, because of the gastric delights she fabricates in these and because the more they're used the better seasoned they become, I've never protested. I simply make sure they're back in the pot box, come spring. Our portable camp kitchen is the frequent victim of raids for such household shortages as paper towels, napkins, salt, and pepper. Replacing these can be overlooked easily.

Compiling a check list can be simplified somewhat by breaking it down into departments. For example, inventory separately the contents of the portable camp kitchen, making sure that all items are in their proper place. A second list may include cooking gear which might not usually be toted in the camp kitchen—such utensils as broilers, frying pans, or folding oven. Another sub-list may tally foods to be taken along and still another, foods to be purchased en route. Checking your list against similar lists published in camping books and various other outdoor publications may suggest some new and useful items to be added.

The most carefully compiled list won't eliminate oversights, however, unless items are checked as they are actually loaded into the car or trailer. It's useless to check them off weeks before departure when you've acquired the items or when you make a mental note to include them.

When packing the car, remember the need for getting at the grub box for a luncheon stop en route. Juggling the tent or an outboard motor in order to reach the sandwiches will contribute little to the congeniality of a picnic. And, of course, if food is to be heated for the lunch, the camp stove and fuel must be equally accessible.

For overnight stops it's also important that the car or trailer be loaded so that cooking gear and food can be unloaded first. Too many campers unload gear at random, struggle with the tent, blow up air mattresses, unroll sleeping bags, gather firewood and water, and inevitably end up eating and doing dishes after dark. Following a late afternoon arrival, get the cook into business first. Unload the camp kitchen and cook kit, bring in water, and light the fire or camp stove so that supper preparations can get under way while the rest of the crew pitches camp. Dad and the older children can rig the tent while youngsters perform simpler chores. If timing is right and the work allotted so that Mom doesn't have to stop to hold a tent pole while the soup boils over, supper will be ready about the time camp is snug for the night.

In order to spring away quickly in the morning, map-eaters are likely to set up a bare minimum of equipment for overnight stops, often taking their meals off the tail-gate of the station wagon by lantern light. It used to be that a camper *had* to be miserable, at least part of the time, in order to enjoy camping, but this is no longer nec-essary nor advisable. Take sufficient time to prepare and enjoy leisurely meals. The Grand Canyon will be there awaiting you, even if you're an hour behind schedule, and its colors all the more glorious if not viewed through the green haze of a stomach upset.

Probably the greatest pleasure comes from setting up an outfit for a prolonged stay. Knowing that you won't have to pull up stakes at the crack of dawn will release a flow of inventive and ingenious ideas for devising rustic comforts and aids to camp cooking. The best campsite my family ever enjoyed was one in Maine where we spent three months under canvas on one site. By the time our vacation ended, we'd erected every known camping and outdoor cooking device, including a lashed Chippewa kitchen, a bean hole, a 2-cord wood rick, log sawhorse, a canopied dining and cooking area, and a 4-foot fireplace to accommodate my giant reflector oven.

In setting up a semipermanent camp, other facets be-sides those of cooking need consideration, of course, in-cluding site exposure to wind, sun, and scenic view; grouping about the fireplace for evening campfires; access to roads; proximity to neighbors; availability of wood and water. However, like general trip planning, these aspects are well covered in other works and our concern is with setting up an efficient camp kitchen and dining area.

The general layout will vary, depending upon whether most of the cooking is to be done over an open fire or on a camp stove. In the latter case, concentrating the kitchen facilities and picnic table under a canopy or fly that is at-tached or adjacent to the shelter is generally good planning. The camp cook is protected from sun, wind, and rain, and the family, too, can dine in comparative comfort.

Whether such a dining fly is attached to the camping shelter or is mounted separately, it will require telescoping or sectional poles of aluminum or steel. Either is satisfactory and the price differential is slight. Steel poles, however, will weigh more than three times the weight of aluminum poles. A 12- by 16-foot fly will usually require four poles to each side, plus two longer end poles and a horizontal ridge. In addition, guy lines and stakes, one for each pole, will be needed.

As to fabrics, the much-touted synthetics are not proving successful since they tend to stretch or "bag" permanently when water pockets develop on the comparatively flat roof pitch. Experiments are still under way, seeking to perfect these delightfully lightweight fabrics, but at this writing, cotton fabrics remain superior. These include a dry-finish drill weighing about 8 ounces per square yard and known sometimes as "Cougar Cloth." Another excellent canopy material is Mountain Cloth, a poplin weighing slightly more than 6½ ounces per square yard, and costing only a few cents more per yard than drill. Even less expensive is paraffin-treated drill.

The principles of efficient kitchen planning in camp are the same as in the construction of a new home. Keep the kitchen area compact, with the stove, portable camp kitchen, and grub supply all within easy reach, thus eliminating unnecessary walking by the cook. Take along a folding table on which the cook can lay out his gear and mix ingredients without interference. A picnic table cluttered with a lantern, beach ball, fishing tackle, badminton net, outboard motor parts, and bird manuals will relegate the cook to biscuit batter on a nearby stump. He deserves better treatment than that.

If cooking is to be done over an open fire, the same principles apply, of course, except that equipment and supplies should be grouped about the fireplace. Rig the canopy so that one edge is close to the fire, but not so close that sparks will light on it.

To one side of the fireplace, set up a wood rick—two 4-foot stakes, 4 or 5 feet apart with twin runners between them—on which to stack fuel wood to keep it off the ground. Sort the tinder, kindling, and fuel. When the biscuits reach a critical point the cook shouldn't have to paw through a pile of cedar to reach a few sticks of maple. Birch bark, plastic sheeting, or canvas should cover the wood pile even in good weather so that a sudden shower won't soak it. The old woodsman's trick of stashing a small supply of dry tinder and kindling in his tent is still a bit of camping wisdom.

Among some campers, the cook rustles his own wood or maintains the camp stove, but in the case of family camping where Mom is likely to be the cook, such chores should be assigned to male members of the family. The camp stove should be refueled daily lest it run short during a meal. If cooking is over a wood fire, the wood supply should be renewed each day before other camping activities get under way. Wood should not be chopped or split near the fireplace. The least that can happen will be chips in the stew, but it might well mean a chunk of wood striking and spilling a pot, or worse still, hitting a camper. Set up the "wood yard" at a safe distance.

Insects, especially so-called "house flies," are attracted to campsites, particularly those which have been in use for some time. These pests appear to have developed an immunity to modern insecticides. Instead of spraying futilely, set up a fly trap made of a glass jar with a conical wire screening entrance in the cover. A bit of ripe meat or fish in the jar entices flies to enter the trap and a small area can be kept reasonably clear of them.

Washing dishes promptly after each meal and keeping all foods under cover will help cut down the insect population. Grease spots on the table should be washed out and bits of food picked up from the ground to discourage not only flies but also visits by raccoons and skunks. Dishwater should never be discarded indiscriminately at the edge of a campsite, but rather, it should be poured into a pit and covered with an inch or so of soil. In those areas where pits may not be dug, it's well to dispose of such refuse water in the sewage system. Rinse the dishpan well with hot water.

Garbage should never be burned in the fireplace. The

17

usual cooking fire will not completely consume such refuse and the stench of simmering garbage won't endear you to your camping neighbors. Deposit all rubbish and garbage in containers provided for such a purpose, always replacing the covers.

One of the charming traditions of the Big Woods is that the cook never has to do dishes. If ever outdoor chefs organize into an Amalgamated Union of Camping Cooks, Chefs, and Cuisiniers of America, this stipulation should be in every contract. Camp cooking *is* fun but everyone who has ever tried it will agree that a camping chef operates under pressure. He contends with the vagaries of a campfire or the quirks of a camp stove; he dashes cold water into the coffee; turns the steaks; sets back the biscuits; lifts out the potatoes; salad dresses the vegetables—all at precisely the correct moment. And, with every meal, three times daily, he faces, squarely and alone, his own personal moment of truth when tongue, palate, and denture contact his handiwork. If there follow the licking of chops, the smacking of lips, the grunts of delight and Arab-like belches of gastronomical fulfillment, he's entitled to sit back and relax—while someone else cleans up the mess!

Chapter II

Firewoods,
Fireplaces,
Firebuilding

WOMEN, more than men, are likely to look askance upon campfire cooking. This is especially true of newcomers to family camping. They envision themselves kneeling on the ground, fingernails begrimed, face smudged with soot, eyes smarting from smoke. It's easy to convince them that the only way to prepare camp meals is on a camp stove. Yet, when taught how to handle a cooking fire properly, women become enthusiastic boosters of the blackened pot!

This isn't to suggest that camp stoves be discarded. Nevertheless, the camp stove has not been invented that will match the speed and efficiency of an open fire when it comes to getting meals. Not only is the fire faster, but larger quantities and a greater variety of foods can be prepared simultaneously.

An open fire isn't always possible. In some regions, where forests are particularly susceptible to fire, open blazes may be permanently or seasonally prohibited. There is also the growing problem of supply in heavily used camping areas to which firewood must be hauled for campers' use. Frequently some of the cost of such firewood is recouped by selling it at "25c a bundle." Our forest lands are still vast, and, in many instances, the annual growth is greater than the cut. We are *not* facing a firewood shortage as such. It's simply that fuelwood too often is not conveniently where the campers are!

On the other hand, many regions offer fuelwoods varied enough to delight the heart of the fussiest camp cook. The camp chef fortunate enough to vacation in such country

19

will ease his chores and upgrade his meals by learning the subtle differences among wood species. With a little assiduous application, plus a tree manual and a little experience, anyone can learn quickly to recognize the various fuelwoods at a glance.

FIREWOODS

For any kind of a fire you'll need tinder such as the bark of the white birch, which will burn fiercely when green or wet. The *outer* bark is the most flammable. It can be peeled easily but should never be stripped from a live tree to leave a permanent and very ugly scar. Unfortunately, the range of white birch is limited to the Northern states and Canada. However, the seasoned bark of almost any tree, particularly that of evergreens, will serve well if dry and brittle enough to crumple under hand pressure. The best among these is cedar. Dry twigs—they must snap and break easily, not bend; wild grass or hay; hardwood leaves; evergreen cones and needles that have dried; palmetto fans; cactus spines and sagebrush—all are adequate tinders. The interior of a "dry stub"—a dead tree that remains standing—will yield powder-dry tinder. Shavings from any seasoned softwood are almost infallible as are the famous "prayer" or "fuzz sticks," whittled from a piece of split dry softwood so that shavings bristle in all directions. Roughly classified, the softwoods are the evergreens and hardwoods are the deciduous trees—those which shed their leaves every fall.

Whittling such prayer sticks or nursing along natural tinders will lend a sense of primitive adventure to firebuilding, but it's rarely necessary in family camping. Such methods are usually emergency measures when more common tinders, such as paper, are lacking. Frankly, I've never felt that a camper should handicap himself by adhering to romantic nonsense such as lighting a fire with no more than two matches or avoiding prosaic tinders such as a discarded bread wrapper! Use whatever inflammables are at hand, be they yesterday's newspaper or an empty cracker box. Wax-impregnated milk cartons burn readily although the more recently introduced plastic-coated cartons burn only reluctantly. "Homemade" fire starters are numberless and include wadded newspaper, cotton wads or bits of porous wallboard dipped in melted paraffin. Candles, dabs of Sterno, Heatabs or Trioxane sticks—all help give a fire a healthy start even in a downpour.

Beware, however, of using liquid flammables such as gasoline, kerosene, or naphtha on a dormant fire under which there may be glowing coals. These liquids vaporize almost instantly and will flare up violently. Never pour gasoline or naphtha directly on flames, no matter how small, since flames will run up the flowing liquid before you can withdraw your hand or drop the container. The blaze will literally leap at you!

Campers who have trouble starting a campfire have usually failed to split kindling fine enough. With a little practice, almost anyone can slice pencil-thin sticks from a dry slab of softwood such as pine, cedar, spruce, or fir. Seasoned, fast-burning woods such as these are best suited for kindling but they also are useful for quick fires of short duration, such as might be used for heating a simple meal or steeping a pot of tea. Woodsmen call these "noonin' fires." Such woods, however, do not produce the long-lasting coals which camp cooks seek for more extensive cooking. Instead they burn quickly and leave little residue.

Among the evergreens or softwoods of this type are the balsam fir, cedar, hemlock, pine, and spruce. All of the others are deciduous trees or so-called "hardwoods," shedding their leaves in the fall. Certain among these will "snap, crackle, and pop," tossing sparks and glowing embers that can be annoying and even dangerous. Among these are cedar, alder, hemlock, fir, pine, spruce, basswood, box elder, chestnut, tulip, and sassafras.

The longer-burning firewoods and those which produce suitable coals for cooking come from among the heavier, slower-growing hardwood species. These are considered ideal since they burn slowly while giving off great heat. Among them are: beech, dogwood, hickory, holly, ironwood, locust, maple (hard), mulberry, white ash, white birch, white oak, and yellow birch. While these are at their best when fully seasoned, some are efficient even when green. Hickory, in this respect, is generally consi-

21

dered the finest of firewoods, followed by white ash, the birches, and hard or rock maple.

Some woods, when green, burn reluctantly. Some, in fact, will do little more than smolder until they dry out. Even in these obstinate woods Nature has provided well since they come in handy as reflector logs, fire logs, or andirons. Such woods include the aspen, basswood, black haw, box elder, buckeye, butternut, cherry, cottonwood, cypress, elm, gum, osage orange, persimmon, poplar, tulip, tupelo, and willow.

It's impossible to draw fine lines between species, however, to classify them as good or bad. For example, easily ignited birch bark is notorious for coating utensils with soot. Hemlock, whose knots are hard enough to break chunks out of an axe bit, supplies the only softwood bark that reduces to coals suitable for cooking. Alder, usually thought of as a nuisance brush, is practically smokeless when seasoned and burns with fierce heat. Poplar and aspen hiss and sizzle when burned green and cast an offensive odor, but when seasoned produce little soot. A round pine log will smolder for hours, but will burn heartily when split. Yellow birch clefts easily when green but is nearly impossible to split when dried.

For "manufacturing" firewood, a bucksaw will outcut an axe four-to-one and with much less effort by the cutter. There are several excellent steel bow saws equipped with rapid-cutting "bushman" or "raker-tooth" blades. The fast-disappearing, wooden-frame bucksaw is still the most compact since it can be collapsed into a small bundle and parts for it can be whittled from almost any piece of hardwood.

A log cut with a hatchet invariably looks as if it had been gnawed by a beaver suffering from a toothache and why so many campers persist in using a hatchet is beyond the understanding of expert axemen. The hatchet's short handle requires that the chopper stand dangerously close to his work, exposing feet and shins to glancing blows. Since the short handle permits the use of only one hand, this glancing blow becomes all the more a probability. The hatchet's traditionally light head will cut into wood fibers only with the greatest expenditure of effort by the chopper. In short, the hatchet is probably the world's least efficient and most dangerous cutting tool.

By way of contrast, a 3-pound axe with a 28-inch handle allows a safer two-hand grip, permits the chopper to stand away from his target, and the head's weight adds a labor-saving impetus to the cutting stroke. The Hudson Bay axe, with its 2-pound head and 26-inch handle, though not as efficient as the full axe, is a far better choice than any hatchet. For obvious reasons, double-bitted tools, whether hatchet or axe, should be avoided except by experienced choppers.

Any normally coordinated adult can become a fairly skillful axeman during the course of a two-week vacation. Such skill isn't a natural knack allotted to a gifted few, and not all professional lumberjacks are physical giants. A knowledge of basic techniques obtainable in any woods manual, coupled with practice, will put you in the expert class more quickly than you might think!

FIREPLACES

Fireplaces in America's camping areas range from ideal to idiotic. Among the latter are those found in some state areas of Wisconsin—consisting of a metal tray perched atop a 30-inch pipe. Almost as useless are those in Minnesota's state parks; steel fireboxes pivoting atop a concrete block 18 inches off the ground. Wood fires are practically impossible in the Wisconsin units (apparently the intent!) while the Minnesota fireplaces are such that cooking is limited to boiling or frying. A fireplace belongs on the ground, a commendable realization that has come to states as far apart as Maine and Oregon, where there are U-shaped, open-front fireplaces over which any type of cooking is possible.

Occasionally, fireplaces are built with chimneys 4 to 5 feet tall and these draw all of the heat from the cooking area into the sky overhead. This handicap can be overcome by placing a kettle of water atop the chimney to cut down draft and to heat water for dishes. Otherwise, such fireplaces are nearly useless.

In primitive campgrounds you may have to build your

own fireplace, either of loose stone or of green logs. Rocks are preferable, of course. They won't dry out and catch fire. However, avoid stones which have been standing in water. Tiny fissures in them will contain water which will turn to steam when heated and possibly cause a violent explosion. In any event, the ground should be cleared of leaves and needles, even if wet or damp, down to bare mineral soil or ledge. This clearing should comprise a radius of some five feet or more. A circular fireplace, about 2 feet in diameter, with stones piled in one or two tiers, is the most common type. One side, left open, allows baking with a reflector oven or convenient feeding of the fire. Another well-adapted unit is the keyhole, a round fireplace with a small extension to one side into which may be raked live coals for slow cooking. In either case, pots and kettles may be hung from a forked-stick crane or perched on a wire grill supported by the fireplace walls.

A favorite illustration in camping literature is the frequently rehashed log fireplace, sometimes called a "hunter's fire" or "trapper's fire." Most artists, handier with pen and ink than a broadaxe, hew the top of the logs so that kettles won't teeter. Such illustrations are typical of the nonsense produced by artists whose idea of "roughing it" is toting their noonday lunches in attaché cases! During some thirty-five years in the woods, I've never seen such a fireplace in use, probably because it would take the average camper some four hours to build it.

A wire grill with folding legs that splay outward for added sturdiness is highly practical, although flimsy grills have a habit of collapsing just before dinner is served. The heavy wire shelf from a discarded refrigerator or kitchen range, set on four rocks, offers an excellent cooking surface. Such grills naturally become blackened with soot and besmirched with cooking grease. To prevent the spread of this grime to other cooking gear when traveling, carry the grill in a flat cloth envelope, easily made at home. In place of a grill, I've known some camp cooks, not overly concerned about weight, to carry a small sheet of ¼-inch steel plate which holds and distributes heat evenly.

Picturesque but less efficient is the fireplace crane—two

green crotches with a lug pole lying in the forks, from which are suspended pot hooks for holding kettles. Invariably, new campers use forked sticks that are too flimsy. Seek out crotched hardwoods at least 2 inches in diameter and 3 to 4 feet long, which are then sharpened at the bottom end and driven firmly into the ground, one on each side of the fireplace, so that the equally rugged horizontal lug pole lies directly over the fire pit at a height of 30 to 36 inches. Pot hooks are also made of hardwood crotches, about an inch thick. Cut several, with the branch offshoot 4 inches long, but vary the length of the stem from 10 to 18 inches. Notch the lower ends of the stems at a downward angle so that kettles cannot slip out. With pot hooks of different lengths you can adjust the height of utensils over the fire. Don't discard pot hooks when breaking camp. They toughen with heating and will last for years. Pot hooks can also be made easily by twisting a coat hanger or other heavy wire into S shapes.

Hanging a kettle from a tripod, so often seen in TV Indian camps, is a waste of effort. Why cut *three* poles when a single "dingle stick," set diagonally in an upright fork, will do the job? The dingle stick is a straight pole, possibly 6 feet long, staked or ballasted to the ground at its lower end to counterbalance the weight of a pot hanging from it over the fire. An old Indian belief is that to leave a "chip-lok-wagan" (dingle stick) standing over a dead campfire is to invite trouble from evil spirits. To this day, you'll find such a stick at campsites in many parts of the North, but it will be leaning against a tree! Horace Kephart, in his classic *Camping and Woodcraft*, points out that the dingle stick is known by some twenty-nine different names!

Despite all the bad jokes about rubbing two Boy Scouts together, you'll need matches for your fire. Matches are like money when you go to the Big City—always take along more than you think you'll need. Wooden matches are still the best fire starters and these can be carried safely in quantity in friction-top cans. For an emergency supply of matches, dip a few dozen in clear fingernail polish or into shellac thinned slightly with denatured alcohol.

FIRE BUILDING

Far too much emphasis is placed on romantically but idiotically dubbed fire structures such as the Teepee, Log Cabin, Hunter's or Trapper's, Lazy Man's, Self-Feeding, Platform, and Altar. As long as this nonsense persists, beginners will have fire-building troubles. Under favorable conditions, almost any combination of tinder and kindling will burn, but when rain and wind set the odds against a camper, the romantic gibberish falls apart at the seams and the frustrated camper wonders what he did wrong. I must confess that I build only one kind of a fire and, somehow, it burns come rain, hail, snow, sleet, or wind.

Successful fire building is simplicity itself. Apart from the frequent failure to split kindling fine enough, fire-building troubles usually result from heaping on wood so that it smolders the tinder, cutting off the oxygen supply. To avoid this, lay a single "base stick," 2 to 3 inches in diameter, in the fireplace. Crumple ample tinder loosely to the *windward* side of the base stick, then place thinly split (¼ to ½ inch) kindling over the tinder so that it rests at one end over the base stick. Light the tinder *as close to the ground as possible* and to *windward,* so that the wind will blow the infant flame *into* the fuel. As the fire starts to burn, the weight of the kindling will settle the tinder, but the former can't drop below the level of the base stick. Air can then circulate freely at the base of the fire. The Girl Scouts now teach a very similar method which they term the "Basic A." The Boy Scouts, according to several complaints I've had from scoutmasters, are still struggling with Teepees and Log Cabins!

Any infant fire faces a difficult and often unsuccessful struggle in a downpour. This problem can be overcome by inverting a small cardboard carton with one end cut out and with a "chimney hole" cut into the opposite end. Build your fire under the box. It will eventually catch fire, of course, but by that time your blaze will have become a robust fire which will need only added fuel to keep it burning, even in a rain. In the north country, a quonset hutlike hood can be made of birch bark to serve the same purpose.

Once under way, heavier wood can be added, this placed in a criss-cross manner to allow passage for upward draft. Placing sticks closely together and parallel—"layin' a floor," I once heard a guide call it—will cut off this upward draft.

The simplest cooking fire is the woodsman's "noonin' fire," just large enough to lick the bottom of the pot. A full-fledged cooking fire is nothing more than an enlargement of this, its size and shape governed by the cooking chores scheduled for it. However, leaping flames increase draft and carry away much heat which scorches foods in its skyward rise. Do not build a fire larger than you'll need.

Chapter III

Camp-stove
Fuels

THE MAJORITY of camping wives and mothers—and they do most of the cooking among family campers—agree that an evening campfire is indispensable to marshmallow toasting. There, however, they draw the line. An open cooking fire, they're quick to point out, is continually in need of lung-searing huffing and puffing, best done on hands and knees; smoke persecutes the cook by following her around; soot smears pots and seems to leap fiendishly to hands and face; rain creates a smudge, wind a conflagration; embers pop into food, burn holes in clothing; firewood is either too wet, too green, too heavy, too large, too far away, or just too much trouble. Daniel Boone, they insist, would gladly have traded his hatchet for a Coleman stove.

An old hand at campfire cooking won't agree, of course, but he's overwhelmingly outnumbered since there's some element of truth in these disclaimers. After all, we're now in our second generation of electronic cooking, TV dinners, and instant spaghetti and meat balls. Grandmother's black wood-burning kitchen range has been relegated to the museum for the wonderment of people who cluck their tongues sympathetically, and the ability to build a fire is as outdated as the wind-up Victrola! In the light of these facts, it's not surprising that the bulk of camp meals are prepared on camp stoves.

Most of these are gasoline-burning types, although "bottle gas," including butane and propane, is making a strong bid to replace gasoline on the campgrounds, as it has in

Europe. In addition, there are stoves that burn kerosene, naphtha, and alcohol. The newcomer to camp cooking, then, is much like the small boy in a candy store with only a nickel to spend. Decisions come hard.

One approach to a decision, I decided, was to determine the heat values of various fuels. A university thermodynamics instructor explained that a BTU is a British Thermal Unit, equivalent to the heat required to raise the temperature of one pound of water one degree Fahrenheit, starting at 39 degrees. He unlimbered his slide rule and came up with the first concrete evidence that campstove fuels *do* vary in efficiency! His evaluations follow:

Fuel	Heat Value Per Gallon
Kerosene	132,500 BTU's
Naphtha	121,000
Gasoline	119,200
Butane	101,000
Propane	91,800
Methyl Alcohol	64,400

At first glance one might make kerosene the first choice but I decided to test the fuels in some 20 stoves before deciding. This led to the discovery that there's more to fuel efficiency than BTU's.

Equipment catalogs rate the heat output of various stoves so that it's nearly impossible to compare them. Some, for example, are rated at so many BTU's, although it is not indicated whether this output is hourly or per tankful of fuel. Others claim the ability to boil a quart of water in a given number of minutes, while a third group uses a pint of water as the standard. Still others are rated as "highly efficient" or attributed a modest "amazing!" My tests consisted simply of timing the speed with which the various stoves, using nine different fuels, boiled one pint of water in a 6-inch aluminum saucepan. The water was at 52 degrees when placed on the burner, which had been allowed to reach its peak efficiency. The stoves tested varied from simple "canned heat" units to elaborate three-burner gasoline models, some new, others as much as eight years old. The results were not flattering to all stove manufacturers, but they did produce a tribute of sorts—not one of the stoves malfunctioned!

The fastest boiling time for each of the six major fuels follows:

White Gasoline	1 minutes	55 seconds
Propane	2	10
Naphtha	2	15
Leaded Gasoline	2	25
Kerosene	3	10
Butane	3	50

Surprisingly, the fastest time was produced on a stove no longer manufactured, a KampKook which I've toted several thousand miles during some eight years; its generator has never been replaced and it has never needed any other repairs. The tests also proved what I'd suspected: that most of the miniature stoves burning so-called "canned heat" are inadequate for any but minimal camp cooking, turning in a boiling time of 10 minutes and 40 seconds. Methyl alcohol proved to be the slowest of the popular fuels, white gasoline the fastest. By way of pointing up the general efficiency of camp stoves, a household electric range took 4 minutes and 25 seconds, which was slower than all gasoline stoves.

ALCOHOL

The alcohol used in camp stoves is known as methyl or denatured alcohol or methylated spirits, probably most generally used as a shellac or paint solvent, and easily available at most hardware and paint stores. Care should be taken that lacquer thinner or solvent is not used. Methyl alcohol is a safe camp-stove fuel that burns with an intense blue flame which creates little, if any, soot, carbon, or odor. However, in view of its low BTU content, inefficiency compared to gasoline or propane, and comparatively high hourly operating cost (10 to 20 cents), it is likely to be the choice of few campers. In testing, alcohol required close to 6 minutes to boil the pint of water.

BUTANE

Butane, like propane, is a petroleum derivative popularly known as "L.P." (liquid petroleum) gas or as "bottle gas." Butane becomes dormant at 32 degrees. For camp cooking purposes, it is packaged only in disposable cans of about 6½-ounce content, under low pressure.

During a Wisconsin camping trip a few years ago, we discovered that Brand X wouldn't fit into a Brand Y stove nor could Brand Y be inserted into a Brand Z lantern. Of the dozen cans we used during the trip, two lasted only an hour each and none burned over 4¼ hours, which, at 59 cents per can, brought operating costs to between 13 and 59 cents per hour, three to sixteen times the cost of running a gasoline stove.

More recently, however, we located a brand whose nozzle is interchangeable among several stoves and whose contents average slightly more than 4 hours per can. Despite its higher BTU content, however, it did not perform as well in the tests as propane, particularly at lower temperatures (36 degrees). It took the stove 13 minutes and 25 seconds—the same stove which had earlier boiled the pint of water in less than 5 minutes at 70 degrees. Butane might be considered adequate for use in auxiliary stoves during the summer, especially in view of the compact and convenient packaging—if its higher cost can be overlooked. At best, however, it falls short of being suitable for any serious camp cookery.

GASOLINE

Despite heavy inroads being made by propane, gasoline is still the most popular camp-stove fuel. The Coleman Company, for example, estimates that there are between five and ten million of their stoves and lanterns on America's campgrounds! This popularity is not without good reason—irrefutable reason, in fact. Gasoline is highly efficient and inexpensive; witness the 1-minute 55-second boiling time by white gasoline in the tests and its 2- to 4-cent-per-hour economy. Also, it is easily available, especially the leaded variety which may be used in some stoves.

Campers, particularly newcomers, are far from agreeing that gasoline is the ideal fuel, despite its popularity among the more experienced campers. Some consider the once-a-day filling of the tank a nuisance, although this chore should hardly bring about any great degree of weariness. Possible spilling of a highly volatile liquid is objected to, but this can be eliminated by careful use of a funnel. The necessary frequent pumping of the tank is also criticized. Women often fear lighting a gasoline stove, possibly having been frightened by a "flare up" or a hair-raising "Poof!" although these are usually the result of improper valve adjustments. Some cussing results, too, from having occasionally to replace a generator, particularly if the need arises just before the pork chops are ready! Beginners are also puzzled by having to manipulate two valves, and some fear carbon monoxide, a product of burning gasoline. Actually, most of these fears or criticisms disappear once a camper is accustomed to a gasoline stove, but to neophytes, they are very real indeed.

White or unleaded gasoline proved the fastest during tests, at 2 minutes, 10 seconds. Leaded gasoline, too, turned in a respectable speed of 2 minutes, 25 seconds. Those who choose a gasoline stove have an additional advantage in that they may also use naphtha as a fuel, or a commercial version such as Coleman fuel.

KEROSENE

In Europe, kerosene is "paraffin," made famous as a camp-stove fuel by early Arctic explorers who invariably carried the famed Swedish Primus stove. My collection includes such a stove. When I light it, I envision myself mushing across the Arctic wastes knowing that night will find me endowed with warmth, cheer, and a hot meal, thanks to my trusty Primus! Actually, few Primus stoves are available and most of these are single-burner models, unpopular among family campers. Kerosene, too, has an oily odor which tends to cling to hands and utensils and which may well taint foods. In addition, kerosene stoves almost invariably require "priming" or preheating. Kerosene was included in the tests because it is potentially the hottest of fuels, but it produced a disappointing time of 3 minutes, 10 seconds.

NAPHTHA

Naphtha is a petroleum distillation, ranked somewhere between gasoline and benzine. There are chemical variations, but the naphtha with which I am familiar in camp stoves is Standard Oil's Savasol. During the summer of 1961, we used an entire 55-gallon drum on our permanent tentsite in Maine whereupon we noted a remarkable improvement in stove performance, not only in our own stoves but also among those of the many campers with whom we shared the naphtha supply. Not once during the season was there a malfunction due to gum, carbon, or clogging. In the water-boiling tests, naphtha ranked only 20 seconds behind the speed of white gasoline and, although this certainly qualifies it as a good camp-stove fuel, its clean-burning qualities made it especially desirable. Unfortunately, it is not easily available in small quantities and few campers will want to buy a 55-gallon drum! Its cost, too, is somewhat higher than that of gasoline.

However, a grade of naphtha is packaged especially for camp-stove use by the Coleman Company. Its cost is considerably higher than that of gasoline, but, despite this, many campers, including myself, keep a can on hand in case white gasoline isn't obtainable, and for occasional use to clean out carbon and other residues which may accumulate as a result of burning gasoline. It is sold in most hardware and sporting-goods stores.

PROPANE

Because it is a "gas," propane is the most misunderstood of the camp-stove fuels although its rapid rise in popularity among camp cooks indicates it may well, someday, crowd gasoline out of the picture.

It has been in use in rural homes for many years for heating, cooking, refrigeration, and even lighting. Campers may have their portable tanks refilled by a dealer in almost every town and city in America. It is nonpoisonous and nonlethal and its escape is easily detected, thanks to a noxious but effective odor. It burns with a clean and very hot flame (reported at between 1,800 and 2,000 degrees). Attesting to its cleanliness, breakdowns or repairs of propane camp stoves are practically unheard of! It has, in fact, all of the qualities to make it the ideal camp-stove fuel, including economy when it is purchased in bulk, refillable portable tanks which bring operating costs to about 3 cents per hour, directly astride gasoline's 2 to 4 cents per hour. Little more can be asked of any fuel!

However, its acceptance on campgrounds is being hampered by misrepresentations and incomplete reporting such as appeared in a 1963 issue of a consumer-review magazine evaluating camp stoves. The review stated that it would take about $1 worth of bottled gas to do the work of 2c to 4c worth of gasoline. The article referred to the use of 14.1-ounce disposable propane cylinders which are admittedly expensive, but which, even at their worst, could hardly cost more than 25 cents per hour. The magazine failed to consider the refillable 5-, 10-, and 20-pound bulk tanks, which, as I've pointed out, bring propane's cost down to that of gasoline. Such tanks were not even mentioned!

The fact is that disposable cylinders do not represent the ideal packaging of propane for camp stoves, particularly since they are susceptible to pressure variations due to temperature changes. The lower the ambient temperature, the less efficient the burner will be. If their cost can be disregarded, disposable cylinders are suitable only for warm-weather cooking.

The most practical application of propane lies in the use of the 5-, 10-, and 20-pound tanks. These have a so-called "10% safety valve" which prevents overfilling, thus allowing for expansion of gas during a rise in temperature. Depending upon the amount of use, of course, a 20-pound tank will last the average camping family an entire summer while the 10-pounder may have to be refilled once.

Although gauges are available, the tank's contents can be measured by weighing the unit, this being facilitated by having the tank's net or tare weight inscribed on its surface. Propane is sometimes spoken of in terms of gallons, at other times in pounds, but it's all the same: 1 gallon weighs 4.24 pounds.

Some confusion may result from hearing the terms "high-" and "low-pressure" applied respectively to European and American equipment. Actually, the pressure within the tanks is the same whether they originated in America or Europe. It's simply that American-made stoves are operated from a bulk tank equipped with a regulator that cuts back pressure to "11-inch water column" or, in other words, to a six-ounce setting. European equipment, on the other hand, operates directly from the tank without a regulator at whatever pressure exists, this determined by temperature. American stoves, as a result, burn more quietly but are more susceptible to wind, whereas their European counterparts are somewhat noisier and noticeably more wind-resistant. One of my stoves, a single-burner model made in Sweden, was tested in a wind tunnel at 50-mile-per-hour velocities that failed to extinguish the burner.

Probably the most serious drawback to propane is the initial cost of setting up, from 35 dollars upward, as compared to a 10- to 15-dollar outlay for a gasoline stove. However, this can be cut by purchasing an "old-fashioned" gas hot plate, still available from mail order houses and from gas dealers. Portable bulk tanks can be attached to these easily, along with some sort of a windshield. Any attempt at improvising a propane stove is unwise. Whatever type of equipment you choose, consult an experienced propane camping-equipment or gas dealer. You will then be assured safe equipment.

Chapter IV

Camp Stoves

GASOLINE STOVES

Four out of five camp stoves in use among family campers are two-burner, gasoline-burning models. Probably their most alluring feature is the low initial cost of such stoves. Only recently a discount house near my home offered a well-known two-burner model for $8.88! Regular camping equipment dealers resent the availability of these stoves to discount houses, particularly when they are retailed at less than dealers' costs, but I've heard no complaints from campers who buy them.

The stoves fold into compact suitcase-like units for carrying. Two-burner models run from 17 to 22 inches in length and weigh between 11 and 18 pounds, while three-burner stoves average 27 to 28 inches in length and weigh up to 25 pounds. Tank capacities vary from 2¼ to 4 pints and, depending upon the make and model, one pint of fuel will last from one to two hours at full burner output. Since these are rarely operated at "full-tilt," this fuel consumption rate can be cut one-third when estimating fuel needs for a trip. Most stoves operate well when both burners are lit simultaneously with only an imperceptible drop in efficiency. However, I have an otherwise fine stove which, when *three* burners are functioning at once, won't produce a respectable sizzle over any of them. This is true, so far as I know, of only one brand of stove. Nevertheless, a demonstration might be a wise precaution when buying.

Detachable tanks usually fit inside the case for carrying and a folding cover with wings serves as a windshield, the latter necessary since even a slight breeze will waft away heat from the bottom of kettles and pots. Generally, kettles 8 to 10 inches in diameter can be centered over the burners. Centering these, if they contain liquids, isn't important, but an off-center skillet may hamper even-heat distribution to foods. Nearly all stovemakers offer folding stands which serve to free the picnic table, an asset to larger familes who need "elbow room" at mealtime.

Several stoves boast individual features such as an aluminum case in place of the traditional steel, for greater lightness; rounded corners for easier cleaning of the interior; a tank which need not be removed for operation though it must be lifted out for filling, but may be permanently attached inside the case; towel racks and hooks for pot holders; and the recent innovation, appealing to women campers, of a two-toned color finish.

Several models are designed to operate on leaded gasoline and they do this with some efficiency, but results are generally better, even in these, if white gasoline is used.

Seemingly inadequate at first glance, several one-burner models are ideal as auxiliaries. It's not inconceivable that, while meat and potatoes monopolize the two-burner stove, you may want to simmer a soup or perk coffee. For such use in family camping these little stoves are ideal as "third burners," to say nothing of serving for noonday stops when unlimbering a larger stove might be awkward. Some of these utilize the pressure tank principle while others, notably European imports, must be primed or pre-heated. They are not as efficient as the larger American stoves, but they're far from inadequate.

STOVE PROBLEMS
AND THEIR SOLUTIONS

Failures in the operation of gasoline camp stoves are actually less frequent than is believed by those who *do* have trouble and, more often than not, are due to human error. During the summer of 1961, I conducted weekly "camp-stove clinics" on a Maine campground during which dozens of stoves were brought in because "they didn't work." Of that number, only one needed repairs. The rest were victims of improper valve adjustment by their owners.

This isn't to imply that the gasoline stove is flawless. It has shortcomings, overlooked or coped with by experienced users, but sometimes overwhelming to beginners. We have already discussed the drawbacks of gasolines as fuel. Not mentioned, however, is the complexity of valve assemblies which balk repairs by all but the most experienced "tinkerers." To the uninitiated, such repairs are impossible. Fortunately, it's a rare occasion when repairs more serious than generator replacement are required.

Most campers soon learn that each gasoline camp stove develops a personality entirely its own. No two seem to behave exactly alike. A knowledge of the "innards" makes it easier to cope with these quirks.

Probably the most discussed part is the "generator," which is merely a chamber over, or close to, one of the burners. Gasoline, under pressure in the fuel tank, is driven into this chamber where heat from the burner changes it from a liquid to a vapor. This vapor then passes on through the burner apertures to be burned. Substances in gasoline which do not burn completely create gum and carbon and these eventually clog the generator. Most camp-stove troubles can be eliminated by annual replacement of the generator at a small cost and involving only a few minutes' labor. A wise camper carries a spare.

American-made gasoline camp stoves are "instant-lighting," which means they require no priming or preheating of the generator. Usually, a starter lever or knob is turned to allow passage of fuel into the generator. Opening the second valve allows air to follow. Once in the generator, gasoline and air mix to form a fine spray which goes on into the burner where it ignites. This spray begins to form before the burner is lit and while the generator is still cold. Once the generator is heated by the burning of the air-gas spray (usually in about one minute), the starter lever or knob is turned off, and gasoline only is vaporized by the heat in the generator.

Campers with new stoves frequently have trouble lighting them. A lighted match applied to the burner directly after turning on the valves may be blown out. To avoid this, listen to the sound of the burner and you will note, at first, that a "dry hiss" is heard. This is merely air coming through which often blows out the match. Before applying the match, wait a few seconds for what may be described as a "wet hiss" or faint sputter. This is the sound of the gasoline spray coming through. Apply the match now and the burner will light.

Trouble occurs when a camper has a match blown out and then struggles with a second and possibly a third. In the meantime, gas has started coming through the burner in excess. Applying a match then results in a "flare-up" as the overdose of gas ignites. Should this occur, turn off the valves and allow the excess gasoline to burn almost entirely away. Just before the flame dies, turn on the valves partially until the burner reignites itself. Once you've acquired a steady blue flame, turn off the starter valve to avoid rapid loss of air pressure in the tank. In fact, adding air pressure to the extent of 10 to 15 strokes of the pump is usually advisable.

Don't overdo the pumping, however. Excessive pressure in the tank will cause the flame to burn away from the burner orifices erratically. At higher altitudes, where natural air pressure may be lower, it's often best to light the stove with only slight pressure in the tank. Otherwise, raw gasoline may flood the burner and cause a "flare-up" similar to the one described above. Such a condition is not usually dangerous if pressure is cut back, as the excess gasoline will quickly vaporize and burn.

Overfilling the tank beyond the manufacturer's recommendations will reduce air space, naturally, resulting in your having to pump the tank more frequently and having the flame leap away from the burner. In filling, use a small funnel with a built-in strainer to avoid spilling and to ferret out impurities which might clog jets. If spilling occurs, wipe it dry before lighting the stove or allow it to evaporate for a few moments.

Another cause of flames' leaping away from the burner is an overly lean air-gasoline mixture, resulting from gum and corrosion at the tip of the cleaning needle, which extends through the vertical line to the bottom of the tank. Clean the needle gently but thoroughly with fine emery cloth. This will require the removal of the valve and generator assembly from the tank—far easier than it sounds. When replacing it, apply a little bar soap to the threads to prevent leaks.

Dirt and burned match heads have a tendency to accumulate around the burner orifices and these will cause a yellow and smoky flame which will embellish pots and pans with soot. By removing the single screw at its center, the burner can be lifted to allow cleaning. An old toothbrush makes an ideal tool.

Whenever the stove is to be stored for more than a couple of weeks, flush and drain the tank or allow a small amount of fuel, preferably naphtha or white gasoline, to burn itself out to prevent or minimize gum deposits which may cause trouble later.

Follow faithfully the directions that accompany a new stove. File these where you can find them readily—not at home—but with your camping gear. The directions will also include the stove's model number, a parts list, and generally an "exploded" view of all parts in correct relation to each other. This makes identification and ordering easy. When buying parts from a local dealer, you can, of course, plunk the stove down on the counter with the sage comment that "it doesn't work" and let him figure out the trouble. However, if parts must be ordered by mail, you can't specify a "thingamabob that screws into the lower dingus!" You'll need a name and/or part number.

You have only to walk through a campground to pick up useful camp-stove tips. For example, one woman who was timid about lighting hers, showed me how she used a waxed straw for a "long match," thus keeping her hands away from the "Poof!" which she anticipated. Even when it materialized only infrequently, she was at ease with her stove! Another camper used Windex spray to loosen grease and grime in hard-to-reach corners. Ammonia, applied with a small paint brush, works equally well. Lining the interior of the stove with aluminum foil does away with much of the same cleaning chore.

Since carbon monoxide is a product of burning gasoline,

a stove should never be used in an enclosed area without ample ventilation. This applies to a closed tent, especially during a rain, which tends to tighten the weave in tent fabrics. Carrying gasoline is safe if common-sense precautions are taken. This includes the use of a suitably designed metal container, clearly marked "Gasoline," not a glass jug which might break, or a plastic carboy which may be deformed by chemical action or the sun's heat. Never fill a portable container completely full. Allow room for the expansion which will take place in the gasoline following its transfer from a cool underground tank to a close-to-100-degree car trunk!

PROPANE STOVES

I've already pointed out the desirability of propane gas as a camp-stove fuel with which some might consider prejudicial enthusiasm. However, I would be either obstinate or stupid if I did not enthuse after using, for close to two years, the four models in my own camp-stove battery. Three of these are Swedish-made, the fourth is the first American-made two-burner camp stove, introduced in 1963. Its efficiency compares to that of household ranges and its design and workmanship has the Swedes looking to their laurels. These stoves are popping up on American campgrounds like wild mushrooms following a warm summer rain in a pine forest! And, it's no wonder.

A propane burner has only one valve. You turn it on and apply a match, much as you would light a household gas range without a pilot. (Camp stoves don't have pilot lights.) If there is fuel in the tank, the burner will light promptly. None of my four stoves has ever failed to light, and I camp some 90 to 100 days annually. No pumping is needed; pressure is "built-in." The inevitable blue flame produces no noticeable soot, carbon, or gum. There are no fine jets to clog and, as widely advertised, there's "no filling, no spilling." Breakdowns and repairs are virtually unheard of—nor is this surprising. A propane stove has fewer than half the parts that make up a gasoline stove and none is as delicate. I'm convinced that it's only a matter of time, possibly a few years, before propane crowds gasoline off the campgrounds. Aiding the present trend in that direction is a Visalia, California firm that offers a kit for the conversion of a gasoline stove to propane.

I was a confirmed "propane cook" long before I conducted my not-too-scientific-but-revealing water boiling tests. These only served to bolster my enthusiasm. Propane's average time was 2 minutes and 47 seconds and its fastest time was only 15 seconds behind that of white gasoline.

This is not to say that all propane stoves are ideally suited to cooking for family campers. As indicated earlier, stoves using disposable propane cylinders can hardly qualify as "ideal." Also, several imported one- and two-burner stoves are without windshields, a decided disadvantage, although they are well suited to use in trailers. When used out of doors, some sort of shielding should be devised. I use a folding aluminum reflector oven which fits perfectly around the two windward sides of my unshielded model.

Like their gasoline counterparts, some propane stoves are shielded against wind by their covers which, when opened, have metal wings which fan out to each side. My own Sievert, made in Sweden, typifies the thorough engineering that has gone into these designs. Although only 8 by 15 inches, the side shields are angled so that a 9-inch pan and an 8-inch kettle may be centered over the burners. The stove's total weight, minus the fuel tank, of course, is a mere 7 pounds! The American-made Humphrey, more recently acquired, is the same size as the standard two-burner gasoline stoves and weighs 17 pounds. A feature that I particularly like is the household-range size of the burners.

After using both European and American stoves rather extensively, I'm not sure which I prefer. Probably on camping trips where compactness might be important in packing, I would lean toward my Swedish Sievert two-burner model and its 5-pound gas capacity tank whose total weight is under 20 pounds. On the other hand, where reasonable bulk and weight are not objectionable, I'd probably tote along the Humphrey and a 10-pound tank, totaling 42 pounds. Actually, family campers need not concern themselves overmuch on the matter of weight, but there *is* a limit to what can be jammed into a station wagon! Inevitably, such matters boil down to personal preference.

ALCOHOL STOVES

The camper choosing this fuel has a choice of three types of stove. One single-burner style features gravity feed of the fuel to a rather small burner whose output seems ineffective for anything more than warming baby's bottle. A second stove requires pumping a pressure tank—the same principle as that of the popular gasoline stove, but without its admirable heat output. The third variety, a two-burner model, has large wadded wicks which hold fluid alcohol in complete suspension so that only the fumes escape into the burner orifices to burn. Frankly, I can rouse little ardor for any of them, although the latter stove might interest a camper wishing to avoid gasoline and propane. It, too, is a Swedish import of quality construction. The shortcoming lies in the fuel, not the stove. One of these might well serve as an auxiliary stove to a camper using an alcohol-burning tent heater, a popular accessory nowadays.

KEROSENE STOVES

I've already described the shortcomings of this fuel for use in family camping and no matter how glowingly I may reminisce about Perry and Shackelton in the frozen wastes, these stoves seldom find practical application on family campgrounds. However, for those who may want to investigate, three firms make similar models: Primus, Optimus, and Radius, all of Sweden. Primus offers one stove that is slightly over 10 by 20 inches and weighs 12 pounds—designed as a "household" stove but adaptable to camping by the addition of a windshield. Optimus and Radius make similar stoves, all three incorporating workmanship which might well be the envy of several American stovemakers.

WOOD STOVES

Remembering the crackle of cedar and its aromatic smoke from many an early morning fire in a frost-beset tent or cabin, I'm easily convinced of the wonders of a wood-burning camp stove. However, in the East, where such stoves are few, I'm in a minority. My wood stove is a Sims, made in Wyoming. There are several types in use which fold into compact, though hefty, bundles, or have folding legs which serve as carrying handles for the solid or non-collapsing type. One of the great advantages of these stoves is that they burn almost any solid fuel including charcoal, waste, brush, or, at their best, wood. In many instances where open fires are banned, such a stove with an easily attached spark arrester may be permitted. Besides offering wondrous cooking possibilities, they may safely serve as tent heaters. All have some sort of telescoping stovepipe, usually about 3 inches in diameter so that, for tent use, a "porthole" of metal or asbestos is sewed into the tent roof or wall. They can be set up out of doors, of course. Nearly all will have a built-in or auxiliary oven, draft controls, side shelves, folding legs—and one even has a built-in tank for heating water!

Probably most famous is the Sheepherder, an "old reliable" of the West and available with various modifications, one of which incorporates an oven at the rear of the firebox. Typical Sheepherder dimensions are 13 inches wide, 26 inches long, and 9 inches high, with weights ranging from 20 to 35 pounds depending upon the gauge of the steel. The Sheepherder is usually non-collapsing with stove pipe and other accessories fitting into the firebox for toting. The Sims, of similar dimensions, collapses compactly into a heavy canvas carrying case with a total weight of about 35 pounds. Mine has been battered over many a tortuous trail, yet still serves me faithfully. Despite its far-from-new condition, I can still manage to assemble it in three minutes.

A recent newcomer is the Raemco with firebox dimensions of 10 by 19 by 9 inches and a total weight of about 27 pounds. It is a solid type with a variety of accessories that include a separate oven, charcoal firebox, extension legs, and—shades of a Rocky Mountain cayuse—a battery-powered spit!

It's not wise to clean out ashes too diligently from a wood burner. Leave a couple of inches to help hold the fire on a cold night. Also, before using it, deposit about a half inch of sand or soil in the bottom of the firebox to prevent its burning out quickly. Once used, of course, the attractive paint finish on some stoves will disappear, to be replaced by rust. Don't worry too much about this on the trail. It'll give your stove that "experienced" look, but, when storing it for the winter, steel wool the rust and give the surface a coating of oil. This is all the care your wood burner will ever need. They're tough!

CHARCOAL STOVES

Probably the worst culinary blight on the American scene is the charcoal barbecue grill which some unknowing campers occasionally tote along. I'll concede that the Coleman oven perched on a gasoline stove is an efficient, if unromantic, combination. Too, I restrain my urge to shoot out those giant camp lights that cause near-blindness among campers unfortunate enough to have pitched their rigs within a quarter-of-a-mile. I'll even tolerate the electric coffee pot that plugs into the car's cigarette lighter. At charcoal grills, however, I draw the line.

My objections are also founded upon the more reasonable fact that charcoal is the poorest of all cooking fuels. It's bulky and dirty. It's slow to ignite and takes a brief eternity to reach peak efficiency during which it belches the stench of brimstone. My most vehement objection, though, is that most charcoal grills provide for broiling meats in a horizontal position which allows fats and juices —which contain all of the flavor—to drop into the hot coals and to ignite. The chef (the cuter the sayings on his apron, the poorer cook he usually is) then squirts water or lays lettuce leaves on the charcoal to subdue the conflagration which is by then well on the way toward converting a fine cut of beef into material suitable for soling a paratrooper's boots. An old rubber poncho would serve as well, at this stage.

Charcoal's only concession toward culinary decency is the basketlike grill at whose sides may be hung wire broilers so that meat is then cooked in a *vertical* position. Dripping fats and juices may then be salvaged for basting or gravy.

TIN CAN STOVES

Almost inevitably, outdoor cookbooks devote space to improvised cooking with particular devotion to "tin can stoves" made from metal containers of various sizes and shapes which burn twigs, bark, bits of wood, and even charcoal. These have their place in scouting where improvisation for limited cooking offers a challenge to youngsters and serves to entertain as well as feed. Occasionally, however, adult leaders get carried away with the novelty of such rigs—like the scoutmaster who proudly demonstrated for me his restaurant-size broccoli can which held four pellets of charcoal and which would, given enough time, heat a can of beans. Family campers will find such stoves fun to use occasionally, but they are generally inadequate. Frying an egg on the hot bottom of an inverted spaghetti can can be termed outdoor cooking only with the greatest elasticity of opinion!

Chapter V

Portable Camp Kitchens

ONE OF MY favorite TV shows was a Western in which a cattle drive had been on the trail during three show seasons, and the last time I saw the show, was yet nowhere near Abilene where the big cattle buyers from the East were waiting with a caboose full of gold. So far as I know, the herd never did get to the railroad, and it's no wonder. Every Thursday night the trail boss and his ramrod were interrupted by marauding Indians, wandering Czarist noblemen, renegade gunmen, alcoholic frontier preachers, and dance-hall girls each of whom really had a heart of gold and managed, somehow, to stray into the path of the cow punchers, there to create a situation that called for "bedding down the herd." As a result, the crew spent most of its time around the chuck wagon drinking coffee poured by a cantankerous but lovable trail cook. These scenes focused attention on the chuck wagon whose stern was bedecked with a chuck box—an authentic replica of the type from which early cattlemen were fed on the drive. Today, similar rigs, still called "chuck boxes" or, by some campers, "portable camp kitchens" are perched on stationwagon tailgates.

Much like their pioneer counterparts, the modern camp kitchens hold at least a part of the food supply, cooking utensils, and tableware, all within easy reach so that meal preparation is neatly organized. This helps attract women to camping. Gone is the hodgepodge of battered pots teetering on rocks that so often typified all-male camping. Feminine efficiency has come to camping.

Several manufacturers market protable camp kitchens, but comparatively few are sold despite the fact that they are fast becoming almost as numerous as camp stoves. The reason is that most campers prefer to build their own. Not only can a "do-it-yourself" box better fit the individual needs of a camping family, but it does so at a considerable savings. Also, it has become obvious that some of these manufacturers are not campers and the do-it-yourselfers are quick to capitalize on the mistakes that have appeared in commercially built boxes. For example, some provided for gasoline stove and fuel storage within the box—a guarantee that food will take on a "high-test taste"! Practical campers know this, and while propane units are sometimes incorporated, it's rare that gasoline, kerosene, or alcohol are.

Commercial boxes, too, are almost invariably built of ½-inch plywood or ¾-inch lumber so that when food and utensils are added, weight is excessive. Quarter-inch plywood will halve this weight yet provide ample ruggedness. One of my camp kitchens, six years old, is of ¼-inch plywood, and while it bears the scars of extensive use, it is still as sturdy as the day it was built. What's more, it weighs little more full than some commercial boxes do empty.

Each summer sees a new crop of home-built camp kitchens on the campgrounds, evidence that more and more campers consider the building of a box an ideal winter's project. Skill as a cabinet-maker isn't required. While other campers will admire a skillfully mitered corner joint, they're more likely to observe the contents and how these are fitted into the unit. Many lumber dealers will cut stock accurately to specifications, and if you can wield a screwdriver, hammer, and paintbrush with a modicum of dexterity, assembly is easy—even on the living-room floor. Some campers are enrolling at local high schools in adult-education evening classes in industrial arts with a camp kitchen as their choice of a project. Thus they have access to fine tools and receive expert guidance.

A professional blueprint isn't necessary, but a working drawing—at least a rough sketch—should be made, including dimensions of the overall box and those of the interior compartments. If you can draw it to scale, só much the better. From this can be made up a bill of materials.

The initial step calls for gathering all utensils, accessories, and foods to be included in the box. Sort these according to size, grouping smaller items like seasonings, salt and pepper shakers, matches, and toothpicks. Next, sort larger or bulkier cartons, such as cereals and crackers; large cans and small ones; and place together awkward items like aluminum foil, wax paper, long-handled fork or spatula, and paper towels. Measure the cook kit, drinking cups, plates, and coffee pot. Lay these out on a large sheet of paper, dividing the groups into compartments which will be incorporated into the box.

Camp kitchens are sometimes built without such compartments, utilizing only one or two simple shelves. If this is done, you're liable to find the much-needed measuring spoon cowering behind a can of string beans, defying you to find it. Contents, too, tend to become a jumbled chaos of foods, boxes and cans, pots and pans, especially if the box is manhandled in its transfer from car to picnic table, or if it's bounced over a rough road.

Attempting to crowd one or two weeks' supply of food into a portable camp kitchen may defeat the purpose of the box—efficiency and ease of meal preparation. Allocate space for two to four days' supply, plus room for longer-lasting staples such as coffee, tea, flour, salt, sugar, pastry mixes, et cetera. With supermarkets spaced but a few miles apart between campgrounds, there's little need for toting mountainous supplies.

Dozens of ideas can be incorporated into a camp kitchen to save space, protect foods, or ease the chore of getting meals. You may want to include a small canister set for flour, sugar, tea, and coffee, in which case square cans rather than round ones increase capacity within a given space. A compartmented drawer will keep table silver (don't take the word too literally—stainless steel is best for camping) sorted. Nesting aluminum bowls, known as "dishups" among Minnesota guides, are lightweight space savers useful for mixing ingredients or preparing salads. A small percolator or dripolator is handy for quick coffee. Paper towels are a blessing and you may want to rig a holder on the outside of the box, to be removed for storage inside during travel. (Incidentally, a wire coat hanger makes an excellent paper-towel holder.) A removable wall-type can opener, as well as a wall bottle opener, may be attached. Leather sheaths, riveted to the ¾-inch compartment walls, will protect kitchen knives—and fingers. By drilling holes in the box walls and attaching peg-board hooks of various types, towels, brushes, dish mops, pot holders, may be hung handily.

We prefer china mugs for coffee and a one-inch-high compartmented drawer holds six of these safely. A fully-enclosed drawer may be substituted, of course, to hold the innumerable small items that tend to stray. We even included a small metal bread box, removable for cleaning. For the awkwardly shaped necessities such as aluminum foil, make sure there's a long compartment—either vertical or horizontal. For really posh late-evening snacks, you can build in a light, either incandescent or fluorescent, powered by the car's battery!

Add a potato masher if you like, but a small soft-drink bottle serves as well as does a quart-size bottle for a rolling pin. An aluminum measuring cup is lighter than a glass one and less likely to break. A simple wire strainer may serve as a colander. Plastic corner clips may be carried in the box and used to tie down the corners of a tablecloth on a windy day. Wide-mouth polyethylene jars are excellent for storing leftovers. An asbestos glove or pot holders should not be overlooked, and, for some, one of those colorful and highly practical plastic dishpans. Since most camp injuries are minor cuts and burns acquired while getting meals, the first-aid kit may be given space in the camp kitchen.

How many added conveniences and luxuries you incorporate will depend solely on your ingenuity and imagination. There is a list in the Appendix directed toward stimulating these.

"Old timers," used to roughing it, will sneer at this posh list and drag in the old cliché concerning the kitchen sink. However, modern family campers, depending upon cars for transportation, may tote along a wider variety of equipment and accessories than has ever before been possible. Since you no longer have to be miserable to enjoy camping, why not take along as many labor-savers as possible? Naturally, not all of the items in the Appendix can be incorporated into any one camp kitchen. They are merely suggestions from which you can make a choice.

Camp kitchen construction details will vary with design but generally ¼-inch plywood is suitable for bottom, top, side, and back panels. For the greatest possible economy, "A-D" grade interior-type plywood may be used. This will have minor defects on one side (it's also known as "good-one-side-only") but these may be hidden by facing them into the box. If "A-D" grade panels are used, be sure that all surfaces, particularly the exposed edges, receive at least two coats of high-grade enamel or marine varnish. Otherwise, the plywood layers may lift or ripple when they get wet. At a little extra cost, marine-grade or boat-type plywood may be used without fear of rippling even if soaked.

Most portable camp kitchens have a drop door which serves as a work area when the box is open. For this, use ½-inch plywood without defects on either side for a smooth and attractive appearance. For a more durable work surface, and more easily cleaned, make the door of ⅜-inch plywood surfaced with Formica or Masonite. In either case, the door should recess so that it fits flush with the forward edge of the box when closed. Hinge it at the bottom with T- or piano hinges. Light chain may be used for holding the door in a horizontal position when open.

Interior partitions are probably best made of ¼-inch plywood although various hardboards may be used. The box itself, if ¼-inch plywood is used, is most easily assembled by means of corner battens of quarter-round stock and wood screws. Amateur woodworkers will find this easiest and affording tremendous strength. However, if you're handy in a woodworking shop you may advantageously assemble the panels with wood glue. Take care, though, that all cuts are perfectly square so that panels will butt firmly. Wire brads or nails are not recommended, since these hold poorly when driven into the raw edges of this plywood.

Rope handles are inexpensive, more "outdoorsy" than

metal ones, and allow the close packing of other items against the sides of the camp kitchen. Simply run the ends of the rope through holes drilled in the side walls and knot them in the interior. Folding metal handles may also be used or, for that matter, ordinary U-shaped drawer pulls. If legs are to be attached, make them adjustable to compensate for rough ground. Campground terrain is rarely as smooth as the floor in a workshop! Hardwood stock, 1 by 3 inches, makes suitable legs, with their length adjusted by means of small bolts and wing nuts run through holes in the legs and in the box's sides. Telescoping tent poles lend a slightly more finished and professional appearance but even discarded galvanized water pipe will do. Some boxes, of course, are used without legs—being set on one end of the campsite's picnic table or on a folding camp table. The latter should be rugged to sustain the weight of the kitchen when it's full.

A BASIC PORTABLE KITCHEN

Camp kitchens may vary all the way from an empty orange crate to a complex, chrome-edged assortment of folding chairs, table, food compartments, all of which fold compactly into the rear of a station wagon or even into the trunk of a compact car. The average home-built kitchen, however, is more likely to be along the lines of the design which follows—simple, easily built, and highly practical.

Even this design, I expect, will be altered in most instances. A national pre-occupation among campers is the observance of other camp kitchens—not with an eye to duplicating but rather to borrowing ideas. The result is that camp kitchens are often marvels of ingenuity. The overall size of your box need not conform to that of my design, but it has proven a convenient size. Anything larger may prove cumbersome when being juggled from car to table, or being set up on its legs, especially if it's well-laden with canned goods. Outside dimensions are 26 inches wide, 21 inches high and 12 inches deep. Depending upon local economics, building cost should run between 7 and 10 dollars, including lumber, hardware, and paint or varnish. When you take the bill of materials to a lumber yard, be sure that exact dimensions are cut and that all cuts are square.

Before starting assembly, cut the ¾-inch quarter-round into four lengths each 11¼ inches. Next, cut 14 lengths of ½-inch quarter-round each about 10 inches but not over 10¾ inches. Note that the top fits *over* the sides while the bottom panel fits *between* them. This is to prevent rain from running into the box should you forget to cover it some stormy night. Using ¾-inch No. 6 flat-head wood screws, assemble the sides, top, and bottom with the 11¼-inch lengths of ¾-inch quarter-round as corner battens as shown in the drawing. Recess these battens ¼ inch from the back and ½ inch from the front edge of the box.

Next, cut two lengths of ½-inch quarter-round 18 inches long and two lengths each 24 inches. Attach the 18-inch lengths to the sides of the back panel, setting them in no less than one inch from each corner. The 24-inch lengths are then attached to the top and bottom edge of the back panel in the same manner. Be sure that these are placed on the surface that will face *into* the box. Use ⅜-inch No. 5 flat-head wood screws. Slip the back panel into position so that it rests against the back end of the ¾-inch corner battens. Drive ⅜-inch No. 5 F.H. screws through the top, bottom, and two sides into the ½-inch quarter-round on the back panel. The top, bottom, sides, and back panels are now assembled.

The two bottom runners, ¾ by 2 inches (not necessarily plywood) which serve to protect the underside of the box, are now attached. The front runner fits flush with the forward edge of the bottom panel so that hinges for the door may later be attached to it. The position of the rear runner is not critical, though it should sit well back to lend the box stability. Attach the runners with ¾-inch No. 6 F.H. wood screws driven through the bottom panel, from the inside, into the runners.

Installing handles of ¼-inch rope is next. Drill two holes at each side, 6 inches from the top, about 5 inches apart and 5⁄16 inch in diameter. Run the ends of the rope (each length about 10 inches) into the box through these holes and tie a sturdy square knot inside the box. If metal handles are to be used, drill the sides to receive short stove bolts. Wood screws, for this purpose, will not hold well in ¼-inch plywood.

Assembling the interior partitions is done *outside* the box. Don't try to insert each panel separately because you won't have room in which to wield a screwdriver! Where a partition corner will butt against the quarter-round battens at the back you'll have to cut a circular indentation as shown in the drawing. A hand jig saw or a sharp pocket knife may be used to cut these. Note, too, that the lower right shelf is indented at one end and the shelf batten under it is shortened accordingly. The chain which holds the drop door open recesses into this notch when the door is closed. A brief study of the drawing will indicate how the interior partitions are assembled. When this is completed, insert the assembled unit into the box and, making sure that all vertical panels and shelves are at the correct angle to each other (90 degrees), attach the assembly through the box walls, top and bottom with ⅝-inch No. 5 F.H. wood screws.

Make the silver tray slightly undersize or sandpaper the side walls so that they will slide freely. The same applies to the drawer under the tray. These may be assembled with wood glue and/or wire brads (No. 17, 1 inch), as detailed in the drawing. Neither drawer should protrude beyond the front edge of the compartments to allow for closing the drop-door.

Lay the assembled unit on its back and insert the door. This should fit flush with the outside edge of the box but not so tightly that it binds. Sandpaper its edges if it proves difficult to insert or lift out. Hinges are then attached along the door's bottom edge, the butt end of these screwed to the runner.

Measure and cut the chain accurately so that it will hold the door horizontally when open with equal tension on both sides. Small eye bolts and the chain are then attached. Details in the drawing show how this is done. A small brass padlock hasp at the top will serve as a door handle and as a locking device. The box is now complete except for painting or varnishing.

Before either is done, the entire surface inside and out,

54

should be sandpapered with a fine grit. If enamel is to be applied, plan on at least two coats. For an attractive design you may want to apply a two-tone finish, possibly an apple green interior and a forest green exterior. A long-handled sash brush helps to reach back panels in the interior compartments, or a spray enamel may be used. If the box is to be varnished, first apply a plwyood filler to be followed by two or three coats of high-grade spar or marine varnish. Sanding lightly between dried coats will develop an attractive, high-gloss finish.

BILL OF MATERIALS

¼-inch Plywood
    1 piece 12 by 26 inches (top)
    2 pieces 12 by 20 inches (sides)
    1 piece 12 by 25½ inches (bottom)
    1 piece 19¾ by 25½ inches (back)
    1 piece 8 by 10¾ inches (silver tray bottom)
    1 piece 8 by 11¼ inches (drawer bottom)
    2 pieces 11¼ by 19¾ inches (vertical partitions)
    1 piece 4½ by 11¼ inches (vertical partition)
    2 pieces 11¼ by 13¼ inches (shelves)
    2 pieces 3½ by 8 inches (front and back of drawer)
    2 pieces 3½ by 10¾ inches (drawer sides)
½-inch Plywood
    1 piece 19¾ by 25½ inches (door)
Miscellaneous
  19 feet ½-inch quarter-round (battens)
   4 feet ¾-inch quarter-round (battens)
   2 pieces ¾ by 2-inch strapping (runners)
   6 feet ¼ by 2-inch strapping (silver tray walls)
   2 dozen ⅝-inch No. 5 flat-head wood screws
   3 dozen ¾-inch No. 6 flat-head wood screws
   1 pair 3-inch T-hinges
   1 brass padlock hasp, 2 inches
  36 inches light chain
   4 small eye bolts
  24 inches of ¼-inch rope (handles) or
   2 metal drawer pulls (alternate handles)
   1 box (small) 1-inch No. 17 wire brads or nails

½ pint enamel (interior of box)
½ pint enamel (exterior of box) or
1 pint spar varnish

A worthwhile companion piece to the portable camp kitchen is a grub box, also of ¼-inch plywood. It's almost tradition that campers tote food supplies in a cardboard carton, and invariably during a trip, the bottom falls out, spewing canned goods, potatoes, and onions over a half-acre lot. Even if the bottom holds, squirrels, chipmunks, raccoons, and skunks have free access. Plywood eliminates these troubles.

An ample box for most family camping trips is 10 inches high, 12 inches wide, and 22 inches long, with a hinged cover and rope handles. Two ½ by 2 inch runners, attached vertically on each side of one end, allow the rope handle to nestle between them when the box stands on end to serve as a cupboard. Removable shelves, also of ¼-inch plywood, aid in making this conversion. Construction of a grub box is much easier than the building of a camp kitchen. The sides and bottom are joined by means of quarter-round battens like those used in the camp kitchen. The cover is attached by means of 2- or 3-inch strap hinges held by short (¼ or ⅜-inch) flat-head screws.

Such a box, without shelves, is a blessing for toting cooking gear too bulky or grimy for the camp kitchen, including a folding reflector oven, Dutch oven, wire broiler, skillet, biscuit tin, and other paraphernalia dear to the hearts of camp cooks.

Chapter VI

Camp
Refrigeration

AT BEST refrigeration in camp presents problems—problems which hikers, climbers, and canoemen avoid by steering clear of perishable foods. During an extended canoe trip several years ago, my wife and I spent hours trying to make dehydrated potatoes edible, but we never succeeded in converting them from starched foam rubber pellets, despite soaking them overnight, dragging them behind the canoe for two days, and finally, mashing them with a Hudson's Bay axe. Fortunately, dehydrated foods have improved hundredfold since that day, but family campers are lucky in that they enjoy what wilderness campers consider to be impossible luxuries: fresh dairy products, meat, and vegetables. The presence of children in family camping makes these necessities, and the automobile makes them possible.

Glowing and "woodsy" descriptions of improvised refrigeration are common in camping literature. Obviously, anyone who suggests a brush-covered pit in a shady hillside for a camp refrigerator has never had moldy bacon for breakfast nor eggs prescrambled by a black-and-white woods pussy! In all fairness, though, I suppose I should concede that makeshift refrigeration in camp is better than none though it's likely to arouse little enthusiasm among lovers of good camp meals.

A favorite is the 5-gallon tin partially sunk in a spring or stream and ballasted with rocks to keep it from floating away. A tight-fitting cover is supposed to keep out skunks, mink, fox, and raccoons, although few of the latter will be deterred by such a slight inconvenience as a tight-fitting top! If such a spring is available, a passable camp refrigerator *can* be devised, but its interior temperature will rarely fall below 50 degrees. Another improvised refrigerator consists of an orange crate or similar box, hung from a tree and covered with a heavy cloth kept wet by a leaky can of water suspended over the rig—refrigerating by evaporation. The unit succeeds only as a physical-fitness appliance, keeping its owner on the run refilling the can which, in turn, creates a lumberjack's appetite that can't be satisfied because, by this time, the food has gone bad!

At my camp in Maine, a 55-gallon drum sank into a shady hillside provided crude refrigeration, but then, Maine nights at that altitude (1,600 feet) supplied a natural refrigerant that the day-time sun never fully dispelled. Even at that, we scrimped and saved to buy a propane refrigerator. The frequent suggestion that a pit be dug in a shaded area and covered with evergreen boughs, preferably on a north slope, isn't to be taken too seriously, although it might prolong the edibility of a slab of bacon a few hours. Also suggested are caves, mine shafts, and abandoned wells. Somehow, none strikes a very practical note—not to those campers who have tried them.

It's no wonder, then, that the camp ice chest or cooler is so popular despite its bulk and weight. The better chests will keep foods refrigerated up to four days on one filling of ice. Naturally, the proportion of ice to food, and the frequency with which the box is opened, will affect efficiency. Too, certain insulation materials render better service than others.

Of the three most frequently used insulators, urethane foam appears to be the most effective, requiring a one-inch thickness to match the insulating qualities of 1¾ inches of fiberglass and 1⅝ inches of expanded polystyrene. In testing water coolers insulated with urethane, we found that ice cubes placed in them on Sunday had not completely melted by Friday. Urethane foam is the insulation material found in several of the better camp ice chests.

Modern chests have outside casings of enamel-coated steel, or of aluminum or high-impact polystyrene, the latter not as susceptible to damage as expanded polystyrene, which is also used as insulation. Liners are most often of plastic, although a few boxes still use aluminum. The best type of liner is seamless and with rounded corners for easy cleaning. The capacity claims of various boxes may be misleading. Some manufacturers proclaim capacities up to 70 pounds, but they may fail to point out that when boxes are filled with ice to such "capacity," there's no room for food! Another regrettable practice applies to what I call "gobbledygook"—the re-naming of known materials such as urethane or polystyrene with confusing trade names which serve only to baffle the camper.

A recent innovation is the inexpensive chest of expanded polystyrene, which, due to the rigidity of this method, needs no outside casing nor inner liner. These chests are amazingly efficient although they are more susceptible to damage from rough handling. Also, raccoons can chew through the polystyrene in nothing flat. Another shortcoming is that food stains are difficult to clean from the interior. Barring these slight deficiencies, however, such chests are fully adequate for camping.

Camp refrigerators are available as horizontal chests or vertical coolers. The latter have the advantage that foods can be kept sorted on various shelves and trays, as in a household refrigerator. Too, ice water is held in a small tank from which it may be drained by means of a spigot without flooding the box—a failing of the horizontal chests. One of the drawbacks of the vertical type, however, is that much of the cold air slides out every time the door is opened, much as it does in your home refrigerator.

The horizontal chest loses cold air less quickly since opening its top cover has little effect so far as the movement of the chilled air is concerned. Cold air won't climb over a partition—witness the open-top refrigerated display cases in supermarkets.

The chests operate best when filled with block ice, rather than cubes. Blocks, however, are not always available, in which case cubes must be relied upon. Some campers freeze one or more quarts of homogenized milk before placing it in the cooler. This doesn't harm the milk if it is consumed immediately after thawing. However, milk that has been frozen tends to sour more quickly once thawed. Water may be frozen in milk cartons or in plastic bags, the containers preventing the water from flooding the box as the ice melts. Commercially available are cans of water, containing a small amount of antifreeze and designed for freezing and refreezing. All of these help keep a chest cold, of course, but campers have several other tricks which improve camp refrigeration.

For example, a chest may be precooled in a Deep-Freeze or walk-in refrigerator before filling it. It is then packed with as large a proportion of ice to food as possible. One pound of dry ice, placed atop 20 to 25 pounds of natural ice will keep the latter from melting until the dry ice has evaporated. Unfortunately, dry ice is not easily obtained though ice-cream dealers sometimes have small quantities available. Care should be used in handling dry ice, however. It is so cold it will actually cause severe burns if handled without gloves. Be careful, too, that an excessive amount of it doesn't freeze food.

Refrigeration engineers are well on the road toward providing truly adequate camping units which operate on propane, alcohol, or electricity. However, presently available portable refrigerators have one drawback in common: limited food-storage space. This shortcoming is minimized by one manufacturer who proudly points to a food capacity of "1,750 cubic inches." Anyone handy with a pencil can quickly determine that this is only slightly more than 1 cubic foot—hardly a spacious compartment. Also, prices of these units start at about 40 dollars and quickly soar up to 170 dollars; a price range that's not likely to start a stampede of campers toward their favorite dealers.

However, credit is due those firms which are trying to produce a satisfactory camp refrigerator not dependent upon increasingly difficult-to-obtain ice.

One of the units finding some acceptance has a food capacity of 1.1 cubic feet, comparable to that of many ice chests. It is available for operation with propane gas in disposable 14.1-ounce cylinders reportedly good for some 70 hours of use. The same refrigerator is offered with a convertible power supply which makes it possible to operate the unit at home on 110 volts to pre-cool it. During travel and in camp, it may then be operated on propane. Another power combination available is 110-volt household current or 12-volt car battery system, the latter using power equal to that of parking lights. The units are thermostatically controlled to maintain a temperature 50 degrees below ambient temperature. In other words, if the outside temperature is 80 degrees, the box interior will be 30 degrees. Another refrigerator offering the same power combinations is considerably smaller, having a food storage capacity of .37 cubic feet. Adapters are available which permit the use of larger, refillable propane tanks.

Another refrigerator which has a 1.1-cubic-foot capacity is one that may be operated on either alcohol or a car's 12-volt system. Power may be alternated between electricity and alcohol, the latter a safe arrangement through the use of a mine-type Davy lamp. All of the alcohol, electric, or gas refrigerators designed for camp use appear to be insulated with urethane foam. As to their reliability, guarantees run from three to five years!

WATER COOLERS

Drinking-water coolers and containers range all the way from the common galvanized pail through vacuum jugs, jerry cans, plastic bottles, water bags, and folding canvas buckets. Pails and buckets, of course, can hardly be considered water coolers and their use is generally limited to toting water into camp. Vacuum jugs have a limited capacity but will keep liquids cool and palatable for up to 36 hours. Jerry cans, G.I. cans, and plastic bottles are strictly for storage and toting, and water held in them for any length of time will become tepid and unpalatable. Desert water bags, popular in the Southwest, cool water through evaporation much on the same principle as the Army Lister bag.

The finest water cooler within my experience comprises a galvanized outer casing insulated with rigid urethane foam and lined with rigid polyethylene. I've used one of these for four seasons, and while considerably more expensive than conventional coolers, it will keep water "spring-fresh" for as long as four days without the use of ice. It's standard equipment on my camping trips.

Chapter VII

Reflector
Ovens

TODAY'S CAMPERS are frequently amazed at the variety of delicacies that are produced in a "new" camping gadget—the reflector oven. Far from being new, in fact, it came into being about 1790, and a frontier log cabin, as well as an Eastern seaboard city kitchen, was likely to have one standing before the fireplace. At first came the "tin kitchen," a round-back unit used for roasting meats on a spit within the open-front oven. The bottom surface curved upward slightly to catch the drippings which were used for basting or drained off for making gravy. The upper half of the rounded back was hinged so that it could be opened without disturbing the oven's position in front of the fire, thus affording the housewife an opportunity to see how the rabbit was coming along. Later came the biscuit oven, whose flat sloping surfaces were basically the same as those in use today, including a shelf on which rested the biscuit tin and its "makin's." Other varieties of ovens came into use, too, including a double-shelf model for roasting apples and a larger oven in which small birds such as quail were hung on wire hooks for roasting. The coming of the cast-iron stove relegated most reflectors to the attic, but not all of them. Early lumbercamp cooks, following the log drive in a tossing wangan bateau, provided hot saleratus biscuits along the river bank, and most recently, northwoods guides made good use of the ovens for feeding hungry sportsmen. Vacationing campers who enjoy open fire cooking now turn out campground delicacies in them.

The beauty of the reflector oven is that it does not require a bed of glowing hardwood coals, often considered indispensable for cooking but time-consuming to produce. Any open fire with a brisk flame is suitable, the theory being that heat strikes the sloping back panels of the oven and is reflected upward from the bottom section, and downward from the upper slope, toward a horizontal shelf on which are placed foods that may range from an apple pie to a meat loaf. To the uninitiated, this all sounds very haphazard. However, during the summer of 1963, I ran a series of tests among several ovens. Using an oven thermometer in a Sims oven, it took only 10 minutes to run the temperature up to 600 degrees before a fire of red oak —not a particularly good firewood! This was the thermometer's limit and, of course, far more heat than is needed for most cooking. There are no bells, lights, or other automatic signals on a reflector oven. The cook has to keep an eye on his production, moving the oven away from the fire when scorching seems to be under way, or closer to the flame if more heat is needed. "Ye cook by guess 'n' by gorry," I once heard a guide explain, but he made the technique sound more difficult than it is. Actually, the oven is remarkably efficient.

A skilled camp cook can match the variety and the quality of dishes produced in a modern kitchen range, although I'll wager that no gleaming enamel range can produce biscuits as fluffy and flavorsome as those turned out before a brisk hickory fire! Probably because skill with a reflector seems unattainable, comparatively few campers use the oven, relying on "store bought" pastries and on fried or stewed meat courses. And—more's the pity— since those who do try it become dedicated outdoor cooks! During camping workshops which I conducted during four summers, I have seen women who could not build a fire on Monday turn out presentable and appetizing chocolate cakes on Tuesday noon! During the rest of each week's course, I was invariably called upon to taste pastries that ran the gamut from gingerbread to peach cake. Anyone having a birthday anniversary inevitably was treated to a double-layer cake, although the "candles" were likely to be Coleman lanterns hung in the campsite during the celebration!

Ovens are generally made of tinned iron, sheet steel, or aluminum and most are collapsible. Metal panels with interlocking folded-over edges are the sturdiest and have no small parts to be lost. Wire pins, used for assembling some models, may be mislaid but this can be averted by attaching the pins to the oven with light chain or wire. Small bolts and wing nuts are lost too easily.

Tinned iron and sheet steel, while more rugged than aluminum, quickly discolor from exposure to heat and, if left out in the rain or even nighttime humidity, will rust. Contrary to popular opinion, even aluminum will discolor to some degree. Keeping these highly polished requires the expenditure of more effort than I care to part with, to say nothing of scouring pads, soap, and hot water. Old-time guides, who used solid or nonfolding ovens, used to flip them over "on their backs" for use as a dishpan, which not only saved toting extra gear but kept the interior of the oven spotlessly clean and gleaming. If this seems highly unsanitary, consider that, after doing the dishes, the guide rinsed out the oven and set it before the fire where it soon heated to temperatures that sterilized it in keeping with hospital standards!

For many years, I argued that a polished interior surface made no difference and, to back up my argument, I often pointed to my battery of five ovens, beaten, discolored, and rusted, with little if any of their original polish remaining. Hadn't I been baking successfully for years? One winter afternoon, when no one else was at home to observe my partial concession, and when my conscience seemed particularly persistent in the matter, I decided to find out how wrong the proponents of bright ovens were. Using a small portable electric room heater as a source of heat, I set up my Sims oven on the kitchen floor. In 10 minutes, the thermometer read 150 degrees. I then cooled the oven to room temperature and lined the interior reflecting surfaces with aluminum foil. This produced 200 degrees in 10 minutes! A shiny oven, it seems, is roughly 30 per cent more efficient than a discolored one, and I was happy to be alone that afternoon so that I could prepare a graceful, if sheepish, admission that I had been wrong for more years than I care to record. I still refuse to polish my ovens. Instead, I line them with foil!

In order to cut weight and so that they will fold flat, ovens are sometimes made without sides. The result is that, when even a slight breeze is blowing, much of the heat is carried away which might otherwise be directed to the food. This problem can be overcome by devising temporary sides of aluminum foil.

Preferably, a reflector oven shelf should be a solid surface, set on wall brackets and well blackened or discolored through use. Such a surface absorbs heat more slowly, holds in longer and distributes it more evenly. The most efficient oven shelf is one that does not extend all the way to the back of the oven, thus allowing for some circulation of heat. This, however, is not a critical consideration. Wire grills or rods, used as shelves in some ovens, expose the baking pan to an overdose of reflected heat and result in the scorching of foods. Baking pans with blackened bottoms are sometimes sold with these ovens but they usually fail to overcome the scorching problem. It's better to add a solid shelf on which to rest the pan.

Ovens vary in size. The smallest unit in my battery of several is one made by L. L. Bean of Freeport, Maine. Its shelf is only 7 by 13 inches, which limits the quantities to be cooked in the oven to a 6-cup muffin tin, for example. However, due to its tiny size the oven sits quite low on the ground and therefore requires only a small fire. Another of my ovens, the Sims, made in Lovell, Wyoming, has an 11- by 15-inch shelf which, while only 2 inches longer and 4 inches wider than the Bean oven, permits the use of a 12-cup muffin tin, thus doubling capacity. The Sims oven stands somewhat higher and requires a correspondingly larger fire. My Swedish Trangia oven with its 8¾- by 18-inch shelf has a top reflector that is hinged so that it can be raised much like the colonial housewife's oven. Ovens with a small vertical back wall allow for the rising of cakes, biscuits, and breads and also permit the use of larger baking pans. Those ovens whose sloping reflector panels come together in an apex at the rear somewhat limit their use to smaller or shallower pans.

While heat is controlled by moving the oven closer to, or farther from, the fire, some control must be exercised over the latter. Soft woods, for example, shoot sparks and may litter food with bits of ashes, and while these will generally be blown off by any breeze, the situation can be avoided by burning finely split hardwood. A good general rule is to have the flame rising to the height of the oven. Don't wait until the fire has died down before adding wood, since it will take a few minutes for the flames to build up again, possibly resulting in a cake that "falls" or biscuits browned outside and gooey in the center. The secret to successful reflector-oven baking is a steady blaze.

Reflector baking and roasting calls for "playing it by ear," especially during the first few attempts. Assured skill will come—and surprisingly soon—but there are no cut-and-dried rules, no exact timing. Prepare meats and mix baking ingredients just as you would for a household oven but disregard the suggested cooking times. Frequently, a reflector may be faster than a home range. You'll have to keep an eye on the "makin's." With most baking and roasting, the oven is first placed close to the fire, possibly within 6 to 8 inches depending upon the size of the fire and oven. As cooking gets under way, set the oven back a little. For example, if the edge of a cake starts to brown while the center is still liquid, the oven is too close to the fire. Most foods will have to be turned once since the leading edge is exposed to the direct heat of the fire as well as reflected heat from the oven. Keep the oven level and facing squarely toward the flames.

Although it's rarely necessary, a fire burning at the base of a boulder or ledge will direct additional heat into the oven. Sometimes suggested is a reflector of aluminum foil, draped from a cross stick mounted on two forked crotches on the opposite side of the fire from the oven. However, I've never found that this heat "booster" is needed.

Rectangular or square pans are better than round ones. The traditional round pie plate, for example, invariably overhangs the front edge of the oven shelf and requires frequent turning to avoid scorching. The hexagonal plate,

67

with its six straight sides, requires less attention. The best reflector-oven pie plate (it can be used for other foods, of course) is rarely seen outside of antique shops or collections. I have one that is 5½ by 13 inches with angular ends that form a parallelogram-shaped container. Its pie-plate lip is marked to guide cutting into six "pie-shaped" pieces! While conducting a camping workshop at the Bangor-Brewer (Maine) YWCA several years ago, I complained to the audience that I'd been unable to find a "square pie plate" for my ovens. One of the women left the room, drove across the city in a blizzard, and returned shortly with the unique plate, which she presented to me. In the confusion that followed the meeting, I never even learned her name, but I'm grateful to her every time I use my Sims oven. Her plate fits perfectly and rarely needs turning. Not everything modern is best!

Another of my favorites for use in this oven is a cast-iron "gem-pan," which my son and daughter picked up in an antique shop and presented me at Christmas a few years ago. The pan is much like a mold for casting metal, except that it casts the most irresistible corn bread I've ever matched to a plate of Maine-style baked beans! When the pan is preheated slightly in the oven and greased very lightly, muffins can literally be seen to rise the moment the oven is placed before the fire! The advantage of cast iron is that it absorbs heat evenly and distributes it through all cooking surfaces. Naturally, such pans are heavier than modern aluminum but the extra heft is worthwhile. Similar though "updated" pans are still available at stores which handle cast-iron cookware. I'm not implying that antique pans are a requirement of reflector-oven baking, however. Pans of heat-resistant glass, aluminum, and tinned iron, or a cooky sheet and even paper baking cups are all suitable. For best results, though, shallow pans are generally preferable, since deeper dishes "shade" their contents from the heat somewhat.

For your initial attempt at reflector-oven baking, try muffins, biscuits, or gingerbread, then graduate to simple cakes—white, chocolate, or marble. These are easier to produce than pies. Prepared mixes are almost foolproof and convenient for camp cooks, but, as I have pointed out, ignore directions on the label regarding baking time. Raised rolls and breads, while not particularly difficult, take more time since they must usually be allowed to rise before baking. As you acquire skill, even these can be produced with consistent success.

Reflector ovens will roast small cuts of meat nicely. The meat should first be seared in a skillet and a small amount of water (about ¼ inch deep) should be kept in the roasting pan to keep the bottom from burning. A shallow pan is preferable and, of course, one without a cover. Frequent basting is necessary as juices will evaporate quickly from an open pan. Particularly lean meats should be draped with slices of bacon or salt pork. With enough time and firewood—and a large enough oven such as my four-foot guide's model—even a turkey or leg of lamb may be roasted, but it's advisable to stick to less time-consuming courses unless you're in camp specifically for outdoor cooking. Small roasts of beef or pork are ideal. Wonders can be worked with small hams, a few whole cloves, brown sugar, raisins, and pineapple sauce. Potatoes and onions, done in the same pan, contribute and absorb flavor. Fish baked in a reflector take on a new and appetizing flavor. A reflector oven will lend stature even to the lowly frankfurt. Slit a dozen lengthwise, stuff with a simple bread or cheese dressing, wrap in bacon strips with toothpicks to hold the latter, and roast in a shallow pan until the bacon is crisp. You'll need the dozen to feed four hungry campers. If you're hesitant about trying reflector-oven cooking on a campground where onlookers invariably gather to scrutinize the operation, practice before the fireplace in your home. Indoor baking is even easier, since there's no wind to contend with. A novel dinner party can result from a dessert—or a full meal, for that matter—cooked before the open hearth.

Chapter VIII

The
Dutch
Oven

HAND-WROUGHT ironware, quite likely including Dutch ovens, was first produced in Massachusetts around 1643. Prior to that time, it had been imported from England. Despite the advent of the fireplace oven and, later, the cast-iron stove, the Dutch oven never fell into complete disuse. It traveled West where, to this day, it still flourishes among pack-train food wranglers. More recently, family campers have become aware of its wondrous possibilities and camping equipment dealers in most parts of the country now stock them. Today's Dutch ovens, though, are made in Ohio and Tennessee, which only goes to prove that the Bay Staters didn't know a good thing when they had it.

The oven I refer to is not the highly polished, cast-aluminum household version with its domed glass cover, loosely termed a "Dutch oven," which is really a mediocre kettle. The true Dutch oven is made of cast iron. The camp cook's model had three short legs, a snugly fitting, flat, rimmed cover and a rugged bail handle—all indispensable to campfire cooking. The legs serve to hold the oven up off a bed of hardwood coals over which the oven is placed when used as a baker, while the cover's flat surface and raised perimeter rim retain glowing coals heaped upon it. The bail is for lifting easily with pot hooks.

Limited use can be made of the older-style, cast-iron household Dutch ovens without legs and usually equipped with a domed cover. These can be used over a fire as bakers and, when set over a camp-stove burner, they produce flavorsome stews, soups, and pot roasts. Most ovens of this type lack a bail handle but usually this can be added easily.

Cast-aluminum "Dutch ovens" are sold by some outfitters, but they're poor substitutes for cast iron since aluminum heats too rapidly, develops "hot spots" that scorch food, and cool much too rapidly when removed from the fire's direct heat. The saving in weight hardly justifies these deficiencies. Cast iron, on the other hand, heats gradually, distributes this heat evenly, and stays hot long after removal from the fire. True, cast iron is too heavy for a back packer to tote, but there's no reason why a family camper can't tuck one into his car. The following chart indicates the relative sizes, weights, and capacities of various camp-type models:

Diameter	Depth	Capacity	Weight
8 inches	3 inches	2 quarts	7 pounds
10	3½	4	12
12	4	6	17
14	4	8	23
16	4¾	12	30

For those less prejudiced against aluminum than I am, there is a 12-inch cast-aluminum model weighing 7 pounds and equipped with a flat, rimmed lid and short legs. A 10-inch version, without legs, nests into the larger oven. That's about as enthusiastic as I can become, however.

The cast-iron Dutch oven is more versatile than the reflector, since it will double as a flavor-retaining kettle and, in addition, it's the equal of the old-time earthenware pot for bean-hole beans. The longer the oven is used, the better its products taste. Perhaps the best way to describe its effects on food is that "it cooks gently." Because of the weight and snug fit of the cover, moisture and flavor are slow to escape, making it ideal for tough cuts of meat such as flanks, briskets, and chuck. It will simmer these gently for hours, if need be, tenderizing as it cooks.

Baking is accomplished by raking out a 10- to 18-inch pad of glowing hardwood coals—the longer burning, the better—from the campfire and setting the oven over these. The oven's legs will prevent the bottom from sitting too heavily on the coals. Softwood coals, which generally last but a few minutes, are not adequate. Coals are then heaped upon the cover with a small shovel or wooden pallet. The cast iron quickly absorbs and distributes the heat of these coals throughout its surface. For beginners, possibly a bit unsure of themselves, an oven thermometer will indicate when sufficient heat is attained in the oven. At any rate, with suitable coals, it takes but a few minutes to preheat the oven. A forked stick serves to lift the cover, coals and all, without the danger of scorching knuckles. The prime secret of success with the oven lies in sufficient preheating.

Much the same advice applies to the Dutch oven as to the reflector. Try some of the simpler mixes—biscuits, corn bread, white or chocolate cakes. Biscuits (dropped biscuits are easiest) may be baked directly in the bottom of the oven, greased slightly. Pies, cakes, muffins, and other pastries should be baked in tins, preferably round ones. Should you find that the bottom of these foods is inclined to scorch, elevate the tins slightly by setting them atop three pebbles or, if your camp kitchen is real posh, on a small trivet. Due to the oven's ability to temper heat, complete failures are rare even among beginners. A wire lifter can be devised for removing foods from a hot oven.

In addition, the Dutch oven may be used for frying and for an unlimited variety of camp dishes such as American Chop Suey, Spanish Rice, Savory Beans, and Chile Con Carne. For this type of cooking, the oven may be hung from a crane over the fire or set atop a fireplace grill. Soups and stews, simmered over a low fire, take on flavor not possible in other kettles! Despite the presence of legs, the camp Dutch oven can often be used on a camp stove by "titrivating" it until the legs fit through the stove's grill over the burner.

The household cast-iron model with its domed cover but without legs may also be used as a baker by setting it atop a fireplace grill over a hardwood fire. Baking, however, should not be done directly on the oven's bottom for fear of scorching. Elevate the baking tin with pebbles or a trivet. Naturally, the legless oven is an ideal kettle for use on a camp stove.

A new oven should be "seasoned" before using, although manufacturers point out that this has already been done at the factory. Additional seasoning is usually beneficial and consists of rubbing its interior with unsalted fat or lard and then allowing the oven to stand at room temperature. Apply the fat or lard lightly as an excess will gather in the bottom. Repeat the process several times. After that, the oven will improve with use.

Never wash the interior with a detergent or strong soap and never, under any circumstances, apply a scouring pad whose abrasive action will ruin the seasoning. If used exclusively for baking, I use only a dry cloth with which to wipe out the interior. Bits of batter that may have spilled and cooked on may be scraped off with a table knife. I have three 12-inch ovens, one of which is reserved for baking, one for casserole-type dishes or stews and soups, while the third is devoted entirely to bean-hole beans. Only the last two get the dubious benefit of hot water. I've heard of camp cooks who also use their Dutch oven for a dishpan; a crime that ranks with the lowest forms of beastly offenses!

A properly seasoned oven will rarely rust. However, should you leave one out overnight (for which a camper deserves to have his oven confiscated) dew or rain may get rust underway. Loosen this with a fine wire pad, rub in lard, and then wipe it with a cloth soaked in hot water. Repeat until the oven is free of rust, then reseason it. The same treatment applies inside or out.

THE COLEMAN OVEN

Probably the greatest boon to family camping cooks—next to the camp stove itself—is the Coleman oven, as easy to use and as efficient as a household range oven. Designed to be set over a single burner of the camp stove, it is equipped with a heat indicator and an adjustable shelf which may be placed in either of two positions. About 12 inches to a side, it weighs 8 pounds, and folds into a compact 12 by 12 by 2½ inches for easy toting. Food may be placed in the oven without lifting it from the stove. It is, in fact, about as foolproof as a camp oven can be with the result that campers who shrink from campfire baking are successful camp cooks because of these ovens. The biggest advantage is that recipe directions as to temperature and baking time can be followed.

The oven may be used over a propane stove as well as a gasoline type, but never in the latter when leaded gasoline is being burned. I've heard it suggested that it can be used over a bed of hardwood coals, but, frankly, I've never tried it.

IMPROVISED OVENS

I once knew a winter-weary lumberjack who improvised a fiddle with an axe handle, some rawhide boot laces, and a motor hood from a broken-down chain saw. He spent several weeks creating it, and had I suspected the hideous mewings that were to fill the camp yard come spring, I'd gladly have ordered a 12-dollar mail-order Stradivarius for him. I feel much the same way about improvised camping and cooking gear. It's rarely worth the trouble. However, campers are inveterate gadgeteers and this trait should not be discouraged completely, so I'll go along with one improvisation—a kettle oven.

Lacking anything else better to do and craving hot biscuits, place a round asbestos pad such as a table hot mat, directly over a stove burner. Over this, invert an aluminum or tinned pie plate—not enamelware, which might be damaged. Place the biscuit dough (or any other dough, for that matter) in another pie plate and set this one atop the first, right-side-up, of course. Now, invert a kettle, slightly larger in diameter than the pie plates, over the latter so as to cover the entire burner area. You now have an oven! It will require lifting the kettle occasionally to check on baking progress but this is easy with a pair of insulated pot holders. Burner settings and baking time will require guesswork at first. Like the Coleman oven, however, this should not be used when burning leaded gasoline. Cakes can be speeded up by inserting a small can into the center of the dough to form a "cake tin" not un-

74

like that used for angel cake. Stiff dough can be formed into a large "doughnut," too, to speed the operation. It works, though, frankly, there was a notable lack of panic symptoms at the Coleman factory when the idea was first proposed!

CLAY OVENS

French-Canadians in the St. Lawrence River valley have been baking bread in outdoor ovens since Montreal was called Hochelaga. Theirs, of course, are large permanent ovens, but a camper with two days' time on his hands and an inclination toward primitive do-it-yourself projects can entertain himself and his neighbors by building a similar oven entirely of natural materials.

A base of flat stones or ledge is preferable, but hard-packed soil will do. Build a rounded heap of short sticks and twigs slightly larger in area than your baking tin and some 10 to 12 inches high—somewhat in the shape of a quonset hut. Now, apply wet clay about 15 inches thick all over the form except for a small chimney at the upper rear and an opening at the front large enough to accept the tin. Be sure the clay is kept wet while you're working and be certain, too, that it contains no appreciable amount of sand or gravel which might later weaken the structure. Allow the clay to dry and harden for about two days, then carefully remove the sticks and twigs that make up the form, pulling them out singly from the bottom through the front opening. If the clay shows signs of cracking, apply another layer about two inches thick before removing the sticks. Next, build a small fire of seasoned hardwood in the oven to complete the hardening of the clay.

In order to heat the oven sufficiently for baking, the fire will need to burn at least 1½ hours, possibly longer. Partially close the chimney hole with a flat rock to slow down the draft, thus retaining as much heat as possible in the oven. To test the oven's heat, rake out the coals but don't discard them yet. Place your hand in the oven carefully and if it's so hot you can't keep it there more than a few seconds, the oven is ready for baking. If, however, no great discomfort results, the oven is too cool. Push the coals back in and replenish the fire.

Set the baking tin on small pebbles within the oven to eliminate direct contact with the hot base stones. This will prevent scorching. While the baking is underway, close off both the chimney and the front opening completely. Otherwise, you'll get a cooling draft across the "makin's." Personally, I think anyone who goes to that much trouble for a hot buttered scone needs a cooling draft!

Chapter IX

Broilers,
Spits,
and Planking

BROILERS

THE FLAVOR of meat, particularly that of beef, lies in its fat and juices. Anyone doubting this has only to munch a luncheon of pemmican. This is meat which the Indians dried in the sun, extracting the perishable juices—a primitive form of dehydration. The meat was then pulverized and fat added as a binder before it was packed in skin bags. However, the Indians frequently added berries *to lend the concoction flavor*. Otherwise, pemmican was a tasteless and highly uninteresting form of trail sustenance only slightly more palatable than snowshoe webbing.

Meat that is broiled horizontally, as over a charcoal grill, doesn't necessarily taste like sun-dried moosehide, but it is distantly related to pemmican in that broiling in this manner encourages juices to escape, dripping to extermination on hot coals.

Broiling meat in a *vertical* position, to the side of a hardwood fire rather than over it, eliminates this. Secondary advantages of this method are that glowing coals are not necessary, a quick brisk fire will do; and the broiler itself often costs less than the meat contents. The prime glory of a steak broiled "standing up," however, lies in the flavor that is retained. The juices must then run counter to the grain, and this slows them. Also, they must run the entire width or length of the cut, rather than merely through its thickness. A larger proportion is then retained. In addition, even those juices which do manage to escape can be saved by catching them in a drip pan for basting. Further, excess fat along the edge of the meat serves to baste it while broiling. This is getting a lot of mileage out of a few ounces of fat and juices, I realize, but meat flavor is like fine old wine. Not a drop must dribble away, either down one's chin or from the bottle cap.

To accomplish this, you'll need a wire broiler which looks not unlike an old-fashioned bread toaster with a long handle. A recent innovation is the basket broiler marketed by Androck in nearly all hardware and picnic supply stores as well as camping equipment dealers. This type is actually a shallow basket and its removable cover can be adjusted easily to accommodate meats varying in thickness from ½ to 2 inches. It can be used for broiling steaks, of course, but also hamburgers, chops, chicken, fish, and even frankfurts.

In the case of steak or chops, place the fatty edge uppermost. If you want to salvage the drippings, stand the broiler up in a shallow pan before the fire, or you can improvise such a drip pan by wrapping aluminum foil to form a tray about the bottom of the broiler. Stand the broiler close to the fire, leaning the handle against a cooking crane, fireplace grill, or prop it up with a green stick.

This will expose the meat to the full cooking effects of the fire without the possibility of soot, ashes, or smoke striking it. The meat will have to be turned occasionally, of course, and this may be done by turning the broiler by means of a forked-stick pot lifter or with an asbestos glove. Glowing coals, which take some time to accumulate, are not necessary. A brisk fire, even of softwood, which can be built up in a few minutes will broil meat nicely without imparting a taste of resinous smoke.

How long the broiler must remain before the fire depends upon the intensity of the heat and upon how well done you like your steak! Pork chops require more time than beef steak, but are especially delicious, since the marvelous flavor of pork fat is retained. Hamburgers acquire new stature and broil quickly. Even frankfurts are tastier—browned rather than blackened. Barbecue and other sauces or seasonings can be applied before or during the cooking process. I've yet to meet an unhappy basket-broiler camp cook. My only regret is that I've been unable to devise a means of applying the method to camp stoves.

SPITS

Back-yard barbecue spits are fairly commonplace, and some are well designed in that they do not broil directly over the charcoal, allowing the drippings to be caught in a tray and used for basting. The same approach should be used with a campfire spit if the drippings are to be salvaged. Mount the spit so that it stands to one side of the fire, *not over it*. A drip pan, or even a sheet of aluminum foil, may then be used to gather the falling juices.

Commercially-made spits for campfire cooking are few. They seem to come and go, none of them finding favor, probably because it's just as easy to improvise a spit with a green stick and certainly much more satisfying. While I disdain campfire improvisations that are complicated and of doubtful value, I go along with the green-stick spit. It's simple and practical.

While stationed in the Maine woods with the U.S. Border Patrol, I once lived for four days on ruffed grouse, roasted three times daily on 5-foot alder or maple sticks over hardwod fires. My pack contained only tea with which to wash down the rather dry fare, but, nevertheless, each meal seemed to be a delicacy!

It's not likely, though, that family campers will be reduced to a steady diet of grouse. Even the broiling of fowl, either wild ducks or the domestic barnyard variety, will probably prove too time-consuming and complicated, since it requires over two hours, for example, to "spit" a five-pound duck. Spit cooking is more likely to be of the shish-kabob variety—easy to prepare, requiring little time, and with ingredients easily available. A typical shish-kabob (more elaborate recipes are suggested later) consists simply of alternating small slices of beef or lamb, potatoes, onions, and green peppers slipped onto a thin green stick and broiled over hardwood coals, or slightly to one side of the fire if the fuel is softwood.

Children particularly enjoy this type of cooking, and their enjoyment takes on a practical note when they are allowed to bake "twist bread" or "biscuit-on-a-stick," nothing more than a heavy dough wound around a 1½-inch diameter stick and rotated slowly by the fire while it browns.

Rigging a spit for such cooking calls for propping a stick by means of rocks, logs, or forked stakes, so that the food overhangs glowing coals or is suspended close to, but not in, the flames. For slow cooking or lengthier recipes, suspend the spit stick between two forks driven into the ground to form a miniature fireplace crane. Don't use softwood such as pine, spruce, fir, or cedar lest you impart a resinous flavor to the "makin's." Maple is probably best, although wild cherry, hickory, ash—almost any hardwood —are excellent. Alder will do nicely. Peel the stick clean of its bark. For a shish-kabob, it shouldn't be over ½-inch thick and, of course, pointed at the upper end so that food particles can be slipped onto it. If you attempt a more substantial menu, such as fowl or game birds, the stick should be about an inch thick. Bind the bird to the stick so that it won't slide around as the spit is occasionally rotated, possibly with a fine wire or by means of skewers.

Some rather complicated broilers, made of twisted pieces of pliable hardwood, are often suggested as well as spits with "natural cranks" for turning. Don't get involved with such nonsense—unless your vacation is a long one!

SAFARI GRILL (or Don't Burn the Funnies)

Strange bedfellows sometimes team up for a common cause. Even though it employs a principle loathsome to my culinary sensitivities, I've found an ally in my anti-charcoal crusade in the form of the Safari Grill which uses, of all things, newspaper for fuel! The day before I tried the grill, Baltimore had clobbered the Red Sox again, and I viciously crumpled the Bangor *Daily News* report, touching a match to the papers as I placed the meat in position over the fire pit. Some 10 to 12 minutes later, I'd been converted from a hard-core skeptic to a nonplused believer and I had a medium-done hamburger that tasted not one bit like printers' ink!

My doubts lay in the low BTU content of newsprint

and it wasn't until I saw fats and juices dripping from the meat that I realized that the newsprint serves as a wick for these and that the meat is, in effect, cooked by the burning of its drippings, pretty well proving one of my persistent but not-always-accepted claims. The hamburger, I must confess, was as good as any I'd ever eaten.

The grill is simply a three-piece "pail," the sections telescoping for easy toting. Draft is provided by holes in the bottom. Four double sheets of newspaper are crumpled tightly and placed in the unit, the fourth lighted as it is dropped. The wire broiler, containing the meat, is then placed over the fire immediately. As the drippings hit the newspaper, these are absorbed and burned. It required four sheets for each side of the meat to attain medium-done status. Apparently, excess fats should not be trimmed. (Remember, this is fuel.) Such meats as lamb, chicken, and pork will require longer broiling and, of course, more newsprint. Lean meats will need to be basted, too. My only criticism of the grill lies with the wire broiler's tendency to spill chops on the ground if not handled carefully, but, quite possibly, the manufacturer has rectified this failing by now. A warning accompanies each new grill to the effect that only black newsprint may be used so—Don't Burn the Funnies. The sports page, I found, produced a better-than-passable hamburger!

PLANKING

It was a U.S. Fish & Wildlife Service booklet that gave me a start when, under the heading of "Planking Fish," it described a 4-pound shad laid out for baking in a kitchen range on a handsomely-finished "plank" equipped with what appeared to be chrome-plated handles. I hope that none of the Service's agents, loyal to it in far-flung wilderness areas, are foregoing the delights of planked fish because they're unable to locate a maple plank with handles!

Planking is for the shores of a lake far from the sounds of man. It calls for a hardwood fire and a good day with rod and line. Too, the plank should be a roughly cleft slab split from a chunk of maple or other sweet hardwood. When exposed to heat, pitch will ooze from pockets in

81

softwoods so, unless you're fond of Trout a la Turpentine, don't use such woods as pine, spruce, or fir.

Instead of dressing the fish in the conventional manner via its underside, slit it along the backbone—after cutting off head and tail—and slice down along the spinal column into the stomach cavity. This will allow eviscerating and cleaning. Wash the fish and wipe off excess water. Tack the fish to the plank, flesh out, with thin nails or, lacking these, wind the fish onto the board with a short length of wire fishline. Prop the plank as nearly vertical as possible a few inches from the fire. Place a strip of bacon along the upper edge of the meat so that, when cooking gets under way, melting bacon fat will baste the fish, keeping it moist and adding flavor. If you prefer, you may brush with butter or margarine. Bake until the fish begins to flake and has turned a golden-brown color.

Chapter X

Skillets
and
Griddles

SKILLET TECHNIQUES

THE SKILLET or frying pan (it's known as a "spider" in northern New England) is probably the most overworked of all camp cooking utensils. Nevertheless, the skillet is well adapted to camp cooking since it is versatile and easy to use, and if the cook allows it to cool once in a while to avoid the monotony of fried foods, it will produce chop-licking meals about which few will complain.

Good skillet technique calls for heat control, an easy matter with a camp stove which is as handily regulated as a household range. An open fire presents problems when it is too large. If only softwood is available for fuel, hold the flames to a low level so that they lick the bottom of the pan but don't climb its rim, curling into it to set the grease afire. Some sort of a grill is desirable for this work and most campground fireplaces are equipped with one. Holding a skillet over the fire by hand invites scorched knuckles and the various forked stick rigs for holding fry pans are the Devil's own tools conjured up by those who never intend to use them! A small folding wire grill is a sound investment for use where fireplaces are not provided with grills.

A hardwood fire is, however, preferable for skillet cooking. I like to let the fire burn down so that I can set the frying pan one or two inches above the bed of coals, propped on three stones or between two small logs. Naturally, the cook who uses a skillet on a camp stove has his problems minimized.

The skillet is probably at its best when sautéeing tender cuts of beef or lamb. This is accomplished by heating the skillet so that it smokes when rubbed lightly with a piece of bacon or suet. Wood cooks are more likely to use salt pork. The fat is removed from the pan and the meat seared quickly on both sides. It may stick to the pan somewhat, but this needn't be a catastrophe. Loosen it with a spatula, fork, or fritter turner. Once the meat is seared, turn down the heat or move the pan away from the center of the fire and turn the meat as necessary until done. Pork, since it requires longer cooking to avoid trichinosis, is not a good choice for the sauté method. It should be broiled, anyway, to be at its flavorsome best.

The regular frying of meats, whether steak cuts, hamburger, or chops, requires a heaping tablespoon of fat or its equivalent in cooking oil. Butter and margarine burn too easily. Although few camp cooks bother, meats about to be fried should be seared, and they should be turned with a spatula or fritter turner rather than with a fork which will puncture it and allow escape of juices. Some meats, such as smoked or cured ham, should not be seared and will require a little grease on a moderately hot skillet. Bacon, of course, "makes its own" and should be started in a cold skillet. Before frying link sausage, I cook it some 2 minutes in ½ inch of water. Some camp cooks allow the water to boil away before frying, but I prefer to pour it off. Not that my method is any more desirable. It's just that I love sausage and usually can't wait. Sausage, like bacon, requires no grease.

A skillet can be an instrument of symphonic beauty when it is applied to hash-browned potatoes, best concocted from left-over spuds. The pan requires just a little fat, and I like to semi-brown a small chopped onion just before adding the potatoes. A medium heat is best and covering the skillet part of the time helps keep the potatoes from drying out too much.

Fish should be fried in a moderately hot pan with just enough grease to keep it from sticking. Wipe the fish dry before placing it in the pan to minimize spattering. Since fish cooks so easily it need be turned but once, browning first one side, then the other. Fried eggs need only low heat and a skilled chef doesn't float them in grease!

Gravy made after frying beef is particularly tasty. Add flour in any amount equivalent to the volume of grease and stir until it is well browned. Then add water or milk, about one cup per tablespoon of flour. Still stirring the mixture constantly, cook until consistency is suitably thick and smooth.

SKILLETS

My favorite skillet is a 9-inch square one, weighing—because it's cast iron—5¼ pounds; hardly a knapsacker's indispensable. Square cast-iron skillets have a twofold advantage over other types. First, the cast iron heats evenly without "hot spots" and second, the square shape gives almost one-third more cooking area than the traditionally round pans. I keep them seasoned as I do my Dutch ovens, and never expose them to the abuse of strong soaps or detergents.

Each of my cooking utensils is associated with some special outdoor cooking treat. My iron spider's specialty is bannock—easy-to-bake and easy-to-eat woodsman's bread which can be made in two different ways. The first calls for a stiff biscuit dough about an inch thick and pretty well covering the bottom of the greased and preheated skillet. Place this over a low burner flame until the bottom is browned and the dough rises somewhat. Then, flip the dough over carefully and cook the other side until it, too, is browned. The second method is for campfire cooking. Place the skillet on hot ashes (not on glowing coals) and cook until the bottom of the dough is browned, then prop the pan as nearly vertical as possible by the fire so that the top bakes by reflected heat. Be sure the dough is stiff enough so that it won't run.

For those who like their meals well organized there is a compartmented cast-iron skillet which cooks bacon and eggs separately, but, frankly, I've never used one. I'm not that neat and orderly.

The "old-fashioned" pressed-steel fry pan is as traditional to camping as the bough bed, and apparently both are doomed to oblivion. Conservation and the efficiency of folding cots decree that bough beds be relegated to the reminiscing of old campers, but there's no justification for doing away with the fry pan. Mine is 12 inches in diameter, but if you want to hold a fish fry during old home week, they're available up to 22 inches in diameter. Such fry pans are inexpensive—the smaller sizes, at least—and practically indestructible, ideal for open fire cooking, or for use atop a camp stove. Some, designed with campers in mind, have removable or folding handles or sockets into which green sticks can be inserted. I rarely use mine strictly for frying, but on a cool day, or when I've some hard miles ahead, I'll whip up a "Slumgullion." Lest you think this is a standard or specific dish, I might point out that every camp cook has his own particular "Slumgullion," no two of which are even remotely similar.

To make mine, I fry a half pound of bacon and then set it aside. Then I pour off the grease, leaving just enough to fry a couple of small onions until they're almost browned. To these I add a pound of frankfurters cut in half-inch pieces and these, too, are browned. Onions and frankfurts should be done simultaneously if they are timed. Two cans of cream-style corn are then emptied over the franks and onions and stirred together while they heat. Just before serving, I sprinkle in the bacon, crumpled into bits, and serve on crackers. I've never had any serious complaints about the dish.

Some years ago, a manufacturer sent me a nesting stainless-steel cook kit of superb quality which included two kettles, a saucepan, and covers which were designed for use as skillets also. The handles were of plastic and removable. At first, I thought the outfit held the answer to the problems posed by aluminum kits, but it proved a bitter disappointment since the covers, when used as skillets, scorched foods without half trying! I gave the kit to Eleanor, my wife, who polished up the outfit, and now it bedecks our kitchen as a handsome and efficient set of kettles—used on a household range where heat is more easily controlled.

The covers of aluminum kits, when posing as skillets,

are Satan's personal abomination—far worse culprits than the stainless-steel covers. I have never used a pressed-aluminum fry pan that couldn't handily scorch any food but water. Some American-made cook kits now include covers of considerably heavier gauge; the manufacturers are apparently trying to overcome the problem. Kits made in Sweden and Japan, however, are usually quite thin and among the worst offenders. Skillets of cast or spun aluminum are a considerable improvement for regular frying or for fricassees, but for pan frying or sautéeing, they fall far short of cast iron's even and gentle distribution of heat.

GRIDDLES

During my first summer as a young guide in the Maine woods, I had thought to improve upon the heavy cast-iron griddles carried by some of the more experienced guides on trips where weight was not a serious factor. Nearly all guides carried one in their boats for lakeshore luncheons although they rarely, if ever, toted them overland. My "improvement" was a cast-aluminum griddle, shiny, efficient-looking, and with only one-quarter the heft of the "outmoded" cast-iron models. I used it once. I'd taken two sportsmen across the lake some 12 miles, then guided them to a hidden beaver bog where they caught trout on every other cast. We had trout for lunch, of course—those that could be pried loose from the griddle! The fish stuck to that monstrous gadget so that they had to be scraped off. It simply refused to give them up! To make matters worse, it warped. My ego suffered, too, since I suspect the sportsmen believed they'd hired the worst outdoor cook in the Maine woods. On the way home, I quietly slipped the thing over the side of the boat into 124 feet of water where, I suppose, great trout occasionally nuzzle it. They had better be careful. Their snouts are liable to stick!

I didn't foresake griddles permanently, however, and my current one is cast iron, 9 by 20 inches, which fits nicely atop a two-burner camp stove or is equally at home on a fireplace grill. I'm quick to forgive the fact that it weighs 8 pounds for the manner in which it turns out pancakes—three man-sized discs of flavor at a time. Of course, a griddle need not be confined to pancakes; it will perform most of the tasks accomplished by a skillet of cast iron, with equal gentleness to food but in larger quantities. For example, it's unmatched as an assembly line for bacon and eggs to feed a family of hungry youngsters each morning.

The iron griddle deserves the same loving care accorded Dutch ovens and skillets of the same material. It will return this graciousness by improving with age.

Chapter XI

Coffee Pots, Tea Pails, and Cook Kits

COFFEE POTS

FAMILY CAMPING has altered the thinking regarding camp coffee pots. During my early guiding days, we had our pots made of tinned-iron by a local tin knocker in one-gallon (16 cups) size, 9 inches in diameter at the bottom. 6 inches at the top, and some 8 inches tall, with a bail handle, friction-fit cover, and instead of the usual side handle, a ring was brazed near the bottom on the opposite side from the pouring spout. With such a pot, a guide could pour coffee with forked sticks without touching his hands to the pot, thus avoiding burns and soot. My wife claims I get too easily "het up" about TV commercials, but the epic that riles me the most is one that depicts a cowboy reaching into a campfire with a bare hand for the traditional side-handled pot. Wyoming Willie, as far as I'm concerned, either has asbestos hands, or he's fond of cold coffee!

While an old-time camper would have snorted at the sight of a percolator in camp, today's family camping coffee pots are more likely to include household-type percolators and drip-pots. What's more, for this type of camping, these are highly practical and acceptable on today's campgrounds. The choice between a "guide's pot" and a more sophisticated coffee maker will depend upon whether the cook prefers to perform over a campfire or a camp stove.

For campfire coffee, the guide's pot has never been improved upon. Its wide bottom not only lends it stability when perched on rocks but also boils water faster. However, you're not likely to find a tinsmith who is tuned up to turn these out. Much to my delight, though, I ran across a commercially made pot almost identical to my trail-battered veteran some years ago—a product of Wearever! This newer version is updated. It's made of aluminum (to which I have no objections in this case, although some camp cooks insist on enamelware); has a glass bubble on the top and a percolator basket which may be removed. I've no idea what happened to the basket but the pot is now in its seventh year. So much is it like my old guide's coffee "kittle," complete with friction-fit cover and a side handle in proper position, that it strikes a nostalgic note whenever I use it. It turns out coffee that brings to my mind tumbling northern rivers, the smell of cedar smoke, and big fish that never get away!

The little 4- to 6-cup aluminum coffee pots with which most cook kits come equipped are tolerable but hardly inspiring. Thanks to a bail handle, they can be hung from a fireplace crane or gin pole, but their vertical sides make for easy tipping and no provision is made for graceful pouring. A few have a ring located opposite the pouring spout, but it's set near the top instead of at the bottom where it belongs for proper leverage.

For campfire brewing in camp pots—which usually come without percolator baskets—"rolled" or guide's coffee is in order. Some mistakenly call this "boiled" coffee. My recipe for it is in Chapter XXIII.

For the camp-stove cook, there's nothing debasing about using a household-type pot, whether it's a percolator or drip-pot, although most drip coffee is likely to taste as if it had been strained through an old horse blanket. I'm partial to campfire coffee, I confess, but there's little wrong with a cup of well-perked coffee. We keep a small percolator in our portable camp kitchen along with a tiny single-burner Swede stove for those occasions when Eleanor and I drink alone, or for those lazy campground evenings when campfire coffee is just too much trouble.

A coffee pot, no matter what type, should be washed and rinsed thoroughly *inside* after each use to be fresh and sweet for the next batch. The exterior of the pot is another matter. Mine has never had more than a lick and a promise applied to its well-blackened sides. This probably contributes nothing to the coffee's quality, but among north-woods outdoor cooks, only tenderfeet have shiny pots. A coffee pot, black as the inside of an infidel's cow, comes as near to being a camper's status symbol as anything I know of!

The mention of instant coffee is likely to bring a sneer to the face of a confirmed "coffee-holic," but frankly, I've grown to like the stuff—at least for quick, on-the-spur-of-the-moment klatches. Certainly, it's convenient, especially for campers, and its flavor is far from objectionable. If you like it and if it's not likely to ostracize you from your friends, by all means take it along. At least you won't have to fuss with a special pot!

TEA PAILS

It was a forest fire warden who taught me about tea and tea pails. On our first extended canoe trip, Eleanor and I had stopped for "noonin'" on the banks of the Megalloway River in northern New Hampshire, where, in my ignorance of the time, the fire I'd built was big enough to roast an elk. The felony had been compounded by my setting the fire against a dry spruce stump, which had started to blaze merrily when around the bend came a canoe, paddled by a grizzled woodsman in a battered hat, checked shirt, and stagged pants, the latter cautiously held up by a belt and suspenders. As the canoe swung into our landing, I noted a fire warden's badge on the suspenders.

"Don't mind a feller steepin' 'is tea," he greeted us, "but ain't yer fire a mite outa hand?" I reckoned mebbe it was, but he waved aside my apology as he poured water on the stump from a large can which he had dipped into the river. Keeping up a running patter about the proper way of "b'ilin' the kittle but not b'ilin' the tea . . ." he rebuilt the fire on more conservative lines, propped a stick over it and hung the can by a wire bail. When the water started to boil, he tossed in a small handful of loose tea and slipped the can down the pole a ways. "We'll let 'er steep a mite," he explained, and without pausing, added: "Nice canoe ye got there . . ." He walked down to the craft, looked it over. "Looks like she's fast," he commented. Then he returned to the can by the fire. "Jes' right," he said. It was. Maybe its flavor is now tinged with nostalgia, but never again has tea been quite *that* good! Instead of a summons to which ignorance of fire laws had entitled me, I'd gotten a lesson in making woods tea.

Not only his technique had enthralled me. His pot fascinated me—nothing more than a No. 10 can (about one gallon, used in food packaging for the hotel and restaurant trade) to which he had added a wire bail. Later, after I'd moved to the "Big Woods," I saw thousands like it making soup, boiling potatoes, and simmering lakeshore fish chowders. Mostly, though, they seemed busy "steepin' tea." Considering the small capital investment involved in begging a discarded can from a friendly restaurant owner, it amazes me that so few family campers own a "tea pail."

Tea-in-a-can need not require bulk or loose tea, of course. Modern, easily-soluble tea bags are likely to be preferred by a twentieth-century housewife whose family has taken to camping. While tea-in-a-cup is most common, tea bags can also be used with the "steepin'" method. At any rate, a No. 10 can that may have held green tomato piccalilli or candied anchovies seems to lend more character to tea!

COOK KITS

The fairest comment that can be made about the nesting aluminum cook kit is that it's a mixed blessing. I've already pointed out certain facets of its cussedness as regards the use of kettle covers as skillets. This dubious versatility has so thoroughly convinced thousands of campers that few remember that covers may also be used *as covers!* An added bit of orneriness, until recently, was the aluminum drinking cup supplied with most kits. It intensified the heat of hot liquids along its rim and burned the lips of anxious users, while the liquid itself went from hot to tepid before you could say, "Ouch! That's hot." Plastic cups are now being substituted and these are acceptable to those who don't mind polyethylene-flavored coffee. As for the aluminum plates, it becomes a race against time to eat a hamburger patty before it cools to a gob of unappetizing grease, its warmth drawn by the aluminum and dispelled into the surrounding air while the eater reaches for the catsup.

The aluminum cook kit is not completely without honor, however. The cups, preferably of aluminum, are suitable for cold drinks and even the plastic variety can be used for picking berries. Too, there's no reason why the plates can't serve as platters for cold foods. It's the kettles, though, that make these kits almost worthwhile.

Cook kit advertising overlooks the versatility of *these*. For example: Apart from being excellent soup and stew pots, one of these can easily be converted to a campfire or camp-stove corn popper. Simply cover the bottom with cooking oil or an equivalent amount of shortening, add corn one-kernel deep, close with a cover, and shake over the fire or stove burner by the bail handle. The oil should be smoking hot and shaking should start as soon as the corn is added.

One kettle inserted into another with pebbles between them will improvise an excellent double boiler with water added, of course, in the larger kettle. They can also be used for food storage and as mixing bowls, water containers, salad bowls, or even as bread boxes. In fact, my daughter once boiled a Maine wildcat in one to obtain the bones for reassembly as a skeleton as part of a high-school natural science project. I could never understand Eleanor's insistence that we never again take that kettle on camping trips!

The kettle comes into its campfire or camp-stove glory, however, in the production of a "one-pot meal" such as American chop suey, chile con carne, savory beans or chowders. True, these are not often concocted entirely in a single pot, since it's a rare occasion when a camp cook—or any other kind, for that matter—doesn't use every utensil he owns. Ultimately, though, all of the ingredients, whether they pass by way of a skillet or a saucepan, end up in a central kettle for final assembly. The secret to easy one-pot meals lies in minimizing the subletting of cooking chores to secondary utensils, but I can't bear to undertake the preliminaries in an aluminum kettle when, for example, I make my favorite corn chowder. Instead, I brown a quarter of a pound of bacon crisp in a skillet. This is then placed in a brown-paper bag to keep warm until needed. Into the bacon grease go one or two onions to be browned. While this is going on, I've been boiling a half-dozen medium Aroostook potatoes, diced into ½-inch cubes, in the aluminum kettle with the cover on to speed the process. When they're done, a can of cream-style corn (for flavor) is added along with a can of whole-kernel corn (for bulk), plus the onions—all of which are stirred together thoroughly as heating starts on a low flame. Milk is then added, the amount depending upon the consistency wanted. I like mine thick enough to be eaten with a fork but my family insists that tradition be maintained and that a chowder be eaten from a bowl. In either instance, I add crumpled bits of bacon just before serving, on crackers, if I've made my point, or in bowls, if tradition has triumphed.

This and other one-pot meals are not for the calorie-conscious or the dainty eaters. They're for campers who've been hiking up a mountain and back down again, or for children who've been rowing boats, swimming, or trying to catch red squirrels with butterfly nets. They're meals for cool days, and it's on such occasions that I feel magnanimous toward aluminum, providing it's in the form of a kettle!

Because cook-kit kettles must nest one within another, most campers try to keep them soot-free, which is easily accomplished if cooking is done on a camp stove whose flame has been kept properly adjusted to a sootless and hot blue color. A kettle dangled over a campfire, however, presents problems to the neat cook. Soot, here, is inevitable. One of the favorite tricks of those who keep their kettles shiny is to rub the exterior surface, bottom and sides —clear to the rim—with bar soap before placing it over the fire. The soap doesn't prevent soot accumulation, but when immersed in the dishpan, the black layer peels off with amazing ease. Soaping is somewhat easier if aerosol-type shaving cream is used in place of bar soap. Some wrap the entire exterior surface of the kettle in aluminum foil. My own kettles get a thorough interior washing, but, for two reasons, I allow the exterior surface to become, and remain, sooty. First, if one of the guides with whom I used to work were to catch me lathering a kettle, I'd probably never again have the courage to set foot in my favorite Maine woods; second, a blackened pot is conducive to gentler and more even cooking. Because of this, one Swedish manufacturer exports to this country an aluminum kettle that has been pre-blackened by the application of a fireproof coating! The kettle is a small one, however, and hardly worth more than 99 cents. Dealers charge 4 dollars. For $3.01 I prefer to blacken my own— over a healthy wood fire.

Sooty pots and kettles are, of course, a problem. To avoid smearing other camping gear, I carry the blackened utensils in individual cloth bags, and for an extended family camping trip I keep the cooking gear in a plywood box such as the one described in Chapter V. During my guiding years, I carried my outfit in a 24-inch pack basket, each utensil encased in a common grocery-store paper bag!

Campers have been convinced that equipment must be lightweight and compact; applicable certainly to the gear carried by hikers and canoemen and then only insofar as the miniaturized and lightened equipment does a satisfactory job. But, why in the name of a broken peavey handle, must family campers conform to this "watch-every-ounce" creed when there are 100 to 300 horsepower under the hood to do the toting? Granted, even a station wagon has space and load-weight limitations, but they're not so stringent that a family camper must forego the convenience and efficiency of somewhat heavier and bulkier equipment. The camp cook who doesn't mind lifting a few extra pounds and who doesn't insist that his utensils all nest one within the other can assemble a cook kit that will ease his chores and make meals a three-times-a-day delight. Generally speaking, most camp cooking can be performed in three basic utensils, a kettle for soups, stews, and casserole-type dishes, a skillet for frying, and a pot for coffee, tea, or cocoa. A basic cook kit need not include *all* of the suggestions that follow but it should be centered about the above three utensils. Whatever utensils are added to this nucleus will depend upon space available in the family care and the extent to which the camp chef wants to let his culinary imagination run.

BASIC COOK KIT

Dutch Oven: Certainly not a necessity, but when you consider that it will do triple duty as a skillet, baker, and kettle, there is no more versatile camp-cooking utensil. A family of four to six persons will usually find the 9-inch diameter model ample. To be used in campfire cooking, the oven should have legs and a rimmed cover as well as a bail handle, while for camp-stove use, a better choice is the household type without legs and with a domed metal cover—not glass. A Dutch oven this size will weigh about 7 pounds and will be worthy of every bit of energy expended in lifting it!

Skillet: Whichever kind you decide upon, don't allow anyone to convince you that "disposable" aluminum fry pans are "just right for camping." These consist of an aluminum frame and handle into which are inserted thin aluminum pans, to be discarded after being used once. Washing dishes in camp isn't such a tedious chore that one must suffer badly cooked food to avoid it! While I prefer my 9-inch square, cast-iron skillets, there's nothing wrong with the old-fashioned, pressed-steel fry pan. A 10- or 12-inch diameter pan is ideal for family camp cooking.

Kettle: The aluminum kettles, whose capacities range from 1½ to 8 quarts and which are included in nesting kits, are excellent. If you're as partial to cast iron as I am, there are available 4- or 6-quart models usable either over a campfire or on a camp stove. These weigh 7 to 8 pounds, less covers. The latter add about 1½ to 2 pounds. Various types of enamelware kettles with capacities of 5 to 8 quarts are also popular. Be sure, however, that yours does not have a wooden handle on the bail, if it's to be used over an open fire. Two minor drawbacks prevail among enamelware kettles. They are easily damaged if liquids boil off and foods stick, and, too, they are subject to some chipping. Swedish enamelware is by far the best, but difficult to obtain. Stainless-steel kettles are also available, but generally expensive and likely to be made for the hotel and restaurant trade, without bail handles. The latter, incidentally, are practically indispensable for camp cooking.

Coffee Pot: This, too, is a versatile utensil in camp, usable not only for coffee, tea, or cocoa, but also for making soups, boiling potatoes, or warming fresh or canned vegetables. I've already described the excellent Wearever pot, and there is also, on the market, an enamelware 6-cup percolator that is ideal for camp-stove use. One advantage of enamelware is that stains can be cleaned easily from its nonporous surface.

Saucepan: Camp meals don't always require a large kettle. A 1- or 2-quart saucepan will get frequent use. Either aluminum or enamelware is suitable. Stainless steel, too. A small kettle is likely to be preferred in campfire cooking, but over a camp stove, the saucepan is handier.

Water Heater: One of the pet peeves—and a just one—of women campers is the lack of hot water. Trying to bathe in a saucepan of warm water is difficult enough, but washing dishes three times a day in a four-quart kettle can well set off a justified temper tantrum! Camp-stove cooks are particularly handicapped in heating water, since the burners are usually busy heating food with no room left for a hot-water kettle. This has to be heated after the meal is cooked and then only in limited quantities. Even if all cooking is done on a camp stove, it's often more feasible to heat water over a campfire where it's just as easy to heat five gallons as five quarts. One way of doing this is simply to keep a 5-gallon square tin atop the fireplace grill, dipping out hot water whenever needed and, of course, replacing it. Gadget-minded campers will like the "water heater" I encountered several years ago. This was a 10-gallon drum which, when I first saw it, lay on its side on a fireplace grill. It had a common kitchen faucet inserted into the upper front edge and a short length of 1-inch galvanized pipe that led from the top (what had been the side vent) almost to the bottom of the "heater." Cold water, poured through a funnel into this pipe, went to the bottom of the tank and forced hot water up through the opened faucet. This arrangement guarantees that there is always water in the heater!

Chapter XII

Often
Overlooked
but Handy...

WHEN IT COMES to choosing cooking gear and accessories, outdoor cooks will range in attitude all the way from the spartan "we'll-cook-it-on-a-green-stick-because-every-ounce-counts" to the posh "let's-live-it-up-at-the-picnic-table"! Somewhere between these extremes, the average family camping cook strikes a reasonable middle-of-the-road compromise in choosing his gear. I suppose there are a few outdoor chefs who will frown on *all* of the suggestions that follow for rounding out a cooking kit. Some may even scoff. On the other hand, I'm sure that no cook will want to tote along each of the suggested accessories. Probably, I'm one of the middle-of-the-roaders in that I've used all of the cooking aids suggested, but never *all* of them during any one trip.

TOASTER

Never having liked the taste of softwood soot, I prefer to dispense with toasting bread on a pointed green stick over a fire. This not only blackens the toast but also the fine name of outdoor cooking. Campfire toast is properly made by holding a slice of bread *horizontally* on a forked stick *over hot coals*—not flames—for even toasting For the camp-stove cook, there are several types of toasters to be used over one of the burners. These include the so-called "teepee" or pyramid toaster, of which there are two versions. One has perforated metal sides (either stainless or blackened steel) in the form of a square "teepee" designed to toast four slices simultaneously. It succeeds at this only if the bread is sandwich-loaf size. The toaster will handle only two of the larger slices. Nevertheless, it produces commendable toast. The second version consists of wire uprights in place of perforated steel sides, and it is comparatively inefficient but can be made to produce golden brown toast if a small metal plate is inverted over the bread while it toasts. There is also a "flat" toaster which holds four slices horizontally over the burner and, so far as I'm concerned, makes far better toast than either of the teepee models. A pound coffee can whose bottom has been perforated makes such an excellent toaster atop a camp-stove burner that a commercial version, square instead of round, is now on the market.

BARBECUE SET

I dislike tainting the aura of camping with the word "barbecue," but this is one tool of that suburban plague that is almost indispensable to camp cooking. True, some campers persist in barbecuing their knuckles by stirring foods with a tablespoon or fork, but only until they discover that torture need not be a part of camp cooking and that a long-handled spoon or fork is far more practical. Forks with handles that extend up to almost three feet are available, but if these prove necessary, the fire is too big! Some barbecue sets include a hanging bar which can be attached to a portable camp kitchen while others are packed in compartmented cloth wrappers. Some cooks like to hang these on a tree close to the center of cooking activities.

TONGS

Every cook on the Maine coast owns one of these for lifting lobsters from boiling kettles, but they also have definite application in camp. Whether you use the spring type or the scissors style, they come in handy for removing baked potatoes from among hot coals or for dividing the meat balls evenly among the children. Some barbecue sets include a set of tongs.

DIPPER—LADLE

Dippers are pretty much out of style nowadays, except on television, when the cowboy in the white hat drinks from one and then dashes the remaining water in the face of the bad guy in the black hat. Among other uses is the serving of soups, chowders, or other liquid foods. A soup ladle is, of course, just as convenient. Either is made in aluminum or enamelware and is so easily stored among cooking gear that it hardly seems worthwhile to struggle with a basting spoon when serving soup.

PUDDING PANS

The uses to which these can be put are almost unlimited. Usually of about 1 quart capacity in aluminum or enamelware, they serve as small mixing or salad bowls, for serving campfire popcorn, for baking scalloped potatoes or meat loaf, as soup bowls, or even as pudding pans! Since they nest compactly several may be added to the cook kit.

COLANDER

At first glance, this might seem ultra-extraneous, but for the family that enjoys spaghetti in camp, the colander is excellent for rinsing—as well as for washing fresh vegetables. Aluminum is entirely suitable but they're also available in enamelware.

DOUBLE BOILER

It's not difficult to justify a double boiler in camp, since indirect heat is best for preparing oatmeal, creamed chicken or tuna, and for certain sauces and puddings. It can be improvised easily as I've pointed out earlier, but since it's a compact utensil which offers two saucepans for other uses as well, a double boiler will pay its own way.

"DISH-UPS"

During a northern Minnesota trip I discovered "dish-ups," and had to acknowledge that a Minnesota guide might be able to show a Maine guide a new gimmick for outdoor food preparation. The dish-up is really a metal mixing bowl and now I have a nesting set of three in aluminum. It's a rare outdoor meal during which I don't use at least one of them for soaking dried beans overnight, mixing a chocolate cake, peeling onions and potatoes, or for tossed salads. Their use is limited only by their owner's imagination and ingenuity and, I suppose, you might even use one for catching a hot biscuit tossed across the picnic table. In fact, the Minnesota guide who first showed the dish-up to me claimed he'd once fashioned a moose-calling horn from one and succeeded in luring a 1,500-pound bull. Personally, I doubt the yarn. I'm sure the bull didn't weigh over 1,200 pounds.

MUFFIN TRAY

This is primarily for use in a reflector oven, although the smaller, 6-cup tray will fit nicely into a Coleman top-of-the-stove oven. Muffins and cupcakes are among the easiest of camp pastries to prepare. Aluminum muffin tins are common in household kitchens, but I prefer cast iron either as a muffin tray or popover pan for camp cooking. Greased and preheated slightly before the batter is distributed in the compartments, it's difficult to effect a failure!

STEAMER

For coastal area camping trips there's nothing outlandish about toting an enamelware steamer—a sort of double boiler whose upper kettle is perforated so that steam has direct access to food placed in it. Clams and lobsters are, of course, prime foods for the steamer, but it can also be used for steaming potatoes, frankfurters, corn-on-the-cob —separately or as a one-pot meal—and it's ideal for cooking spaghetti, since this won't stick to the bottom of the kettle. It can double as a vegetable washer.

FRENCH FRYER

This will bring snorts from those who insist that weight and bulk be kept at an absolute minimum. They can make tea in a birch-bark cup for all I care, but my French fryer goes along! Not that I want French fried potatoes at every meal, but, rather, I'm partial to onion rings! Years ago I worked with a northern guide whose batter-dipped onion rings gained him more fame than did his skill in locating salmon and trout, but, repeatedly, he'd refused to part with the recipe for the batter. Quite by accident, I stumbled upon a package of Aunt Jemima pancake mix in his pack basket. On my next trip, I tried dipping the onion rings in pancake batter and then deep frying them in my French fryer. I'd discovered the guide's secret, and I discovered, too, that pancake-onion flavored "skinny doughnuts" were likely to be consumed voraciously as long as I wanted to stand over a hot fire producing them! Granted, the French fryer has limited use in camp cooking, but for occasional treats such as onion rings or fish, as well as potatoes, some will find it worthwhile. A 2- to 3-quart size is ample for a family of 4 to 6 persons, and the pan itself may be of aluminum, although most guides who use them prefer cast iron. If cast iron is used, the lard need not be changed after each use. Iron, if not exposed to the sun, tends to hold the coolness of night through the day, thus preventing spoilage of the lard. I've known some guides to carry this frugality a bit far, changing the grease only once or twice during the course of an entire season.

CUTLERY

Knives in general, and camp knives in particular, seem to be singled out for abuse. They're often carried in a silver tray or bag where their edges are nicked by tableware. Sharpening stones, for some unknown reason, are a rarity. Knives should be protected by a leather or wood sheath, and a sharpening stone included in the camp cook's outfit. Proper technique calls for moistening the stone slightly with light oil or with water. Hold the blade at an angle of about 20 degrees from the stone and draw it edge-first across the surface of the stone in a heel to tip motion, alternating each side of the blade. One minute a day will keep edges keen.

In the North, a man is judged by the size and shape of his knife—the smaller and thinner the blade, the higher he rates on the scale! A greenhorn stands out like a bull moose in church, for his knife is usually either a Marine bayonet or a commando combat weapon which he wears at his belt in a scabbard and which, if he manages to sit down without decapping a knee, sticks into the ground and hoists his belt up to his armpits! For most camp-cooking purposes, the battery of knives may wisely be limited to household types: a paring knife for peeling potatoes and slicing vegetables, and for cutting meat and bread, a thin 8-inch blade, not over 1 to 1¼ inches wide, is ideal. If a camping trip into fishing country is planned, a flexible-blade fillet knife may be added. Cutting, with any knife, should always be done on a wooden surface, never in a metal pan, since this will ruin the edge.

DISHPAN

Polyethylene is at its best in the colorful and highly practical rectangular dishpans which most campers have adopted. Although they are bulky, they waste little space, since other gear can be stored in them during travel. Some have two compartments, one for washing and another for rinsing. Metal pans are, of course, equally suitable, but the gay colors of the plastic type attract more users. Some romanticists—who probably cook on green sticks and eat from throwaway paper plates—propose that a dishpan be improvised by digging a small pit and lining it with plastic sheeting or canvas, then filling it with hot water! This over-enthusiastic use of shovels is far more harmful to top soils than many realize and is forbidden in most camping areas. Besides, I never liked doing dishes on my knees!

I suppose it's only a matter of time before Detroit comes up with an optional 12-volt outlet on the rear bumper, into which can be plugged a waffle iron, egg beater, or a portable, low-suds-level automatic dishwasher. The list of camping accessories grows longer with each new issue of catalogs, and the wonderful simplicity of camping life is being lost in a jungle of stainless steel, iron, aluminum, fiberglass, and plastic gadgets. All are designed to make life simpler, easier, and more gracious, but usually succeed only in complicating it further. Too, the criterion for determining whether or not these will be taken along is not their practicality or genuine usefulness but rather "if it'll fit into the car, let's take it." I much prefer the formula which leaves behind any item that was not used at least twice a week during any previous trip. More often than not, new gear gets a fair trial at home, before any extended trip, and it should to prove that it will earn its keep!

Therefore, I wouldn't expect that *every* utensil I've suggested in this chapter will be accepted by *all* camp cooks, any more than I'd expect a camper to load his camp kitchen with every item in the list included in Chapter V. In both instances, these are reminders that certain of these accessories might prove useful. And, although I've derided rather strongly some of the nonsensical improvisations that are so popular in camping literature (such as green stick meat broilers!), certain of the more practical makeshifts shouldn't be overlooked in trying to keep weight and bulk at a reasonable level.

For example: for a pastry board, use the work surface of the portable camp kitchen or roll out dough on a clean dish towel on the hood of the car. A biscuit sheet is handy for reflector-oven baking, but what's wrong with using aluminum foil on the oven's shelf instead? Considering taking along a table hot mat? Invert a pie plate. You can eliminate the potato masher by cooking up instant mashed potatoes or by mashing whole potatoes with a small soft drink bottle. For pot lifters, cut yourself a pair of small forked sticks.

If necessity is the mother of invention, ingenuity must be a kissin' cousin!

Chapter XIII

The
Pressure Cooker
in Camp

WHAT SURPRISES me about the pressure cooker is not the speed with which it cooks food. After all, cooking is done with live steam at temperatures ranging from 15 to 40 degrees above the boiling point of water and at pressures up to 15 pounds. What's puzzling is that so few camp cooks take advantage of the cooker's wondrous possibilities which, apart from its speed, include the ability to retain flavor, vitamins, and mineral salts as well as its tenderizing effects on mediocre cuts of meat. My puzzlement is compounded by the fact that pressure cooking is ideally suited to camp stoves whose heat can be regulated accurately. Many, no doubt, are leery of the terms "live steam" and "pressure," but they needn't be. Following the simple instructions that accompany all cookers precludes any danger.

It gives me a back-of-beyond sense of the primitive to impale a shish-kabob on a green stick and broil it over an open fire—a sort of inner retrogression to pioneer days when survival depended upon self-reliance. This is fun occasionally, but there's no need for a camp cook to be a slave to primitive methods. Doing things the hard way, as a regular diet, can pall even on the most dedicated "let's-rough-it" camper. It's equally as much fun—and frequently more palatable—to use up-to-date methods, to say nothing of the time-saving element, which is important when darkness starts to fall on an unprepared supper, or when there are more important camping activities awaiting. Numberless meals can be cooked in a pressure cooker within a half hour, including the time required to set up and light the camp stove.

Fresh vegetables, for example, can be cooked in from 2 to 15 minutes: green beans in 3 to 6 minutes, sliced or diced carrots in 2½, corn-on-the-cob in 5, sliced potatoes in an astounding 1½ minutes! A complete vegetable dinner is possible in less than 5 minutes. As for meats, lamb or beef stew can be ready in 20 minutes. Despite its economy and delicacy, who ever heard of a pot roast in camp if traditional cooking is involved? With a pressure cooker, a pot roast complete with vegetables and potatoes can be on the table in less than an hour. One-pot meal possibilities are practically unlimited.

I can't honestly concede that pressure-cooked beans are quite as acceptable as the bean-hole variety, but the latter require 5 to 6 hours of underground baking preceded by 1½ hours of fire tending. However, soak a quart of pea beans overnight, cook them for 20 minutes with sliced salt pork in the pressure cooker. Then add molasses and brown sugar, according to your tastes, plus a large onion sliced. Heat for another 3 to 4 minutes. Total elapsed time is less than a half hour. The results? Just a *wee* bit shy of bean-hole quality, but that won't keep me from claiming my share!

Frankly, the pressure cooker is not at its best over a campfire. If skilled with open fire cooking, a camp chef can perform wonders with the cooker over hardwood coals, but it will take special attention to the job in order to maintain constant pressure Also, few will want to subject a pressure cooker to the sooting inherent with open fire cooking. With a properly adjusted camp-stove flame, however, there's no soot, and heat can be regulated to comply exactly with cooking instructions.

Nor will you need to hold a stop watch while your eyes are glued to the pressure gauge. Cooking-time tables in instruction booklets may seem inflexible in their recommendations, but the fact is they are approximate. Cooking time will vary according to the tenderness of meats and vegetables. The latter, for example, if fresh from the garden, will require less time than those picked 24 to 48 hours beforehand. The camp cook who deviates slightly from recommendations doesn't necessarily face disaster to his vegetable plate nor to his reputation.

The few existing pitfalls are clearly indicated in the instruction booklet you'll find in your new cooker. Applesauce, for example, should not be made or cooked under pressure, since it will froth and possibly clog the tiny steam vent. Care, too, is needed to bring pressure up gradually in the cooking of such foods as spaghetti, noodles, rice or dried vegetables which, like applesauce, tend to froth.

Cooking techniques are uncomplicated. Insert food and the recommended amount of water in the cooker, close and seal the cover and place over the stove burner to bring pressure up to recommended level. The latter is indicated on a gauge atop the cover. When pressure is sufficient, cut back the heat to a level that maintains constant pressure during cooking time. When finished, certain foods such as heavier cuts of meat may be left in the cooker until pressure drops naturally in from 3 to 15 minutes. Tender foods, notably vegetables, should have pressure cut back immediately, and this is best accomplished in camp by setting the cooker in a pan of cold water or, if available, under a running water tap. Under no circumstances should the cooker be opened before pressure is down. For cooking at high altitudes, additional pressure may be needed. At locations over 2,000 feet, for example, build pressures up to 10 pounds if 5 are indicated at sea level; 15 pounds if 10 are called for. If 15 pounds are required, (the maximum on most cookers) increase cooking time slightly. Some recommend that cooking time be increased 5 percent for every 1,000 feet of altitude above 2,000, but I'd hate to see a slide rule and an altimeter become part of a camp cook's gear. I prefer to play it by ear.

Danger from "live steam" or "pressure"? It's nonexistent if simple directions are followed. All cookers have some sort of a safety valve or fuse which automatically releases pressure should this become excessive, as might happen if the cooker's water content gets too low. Even if the vent tube, which directs steam to the gauge, should clog, the automatic safety release will take over. How often is this likely to occur? My sister-in-law's pressure cooker, which she uses regularly, hasn't popped its safety valve in seventeen years. Probably because I'm too cocksure of myself regarding directions (I'm the type that assembles a "knocked-down" table and *then* reads the directions), my own cooker once popped off twice in one week!

All in all, a pressure cooker and a suitable grub supply can add up to retained flavor and vitamins, fewer pots to clean, more free time for the cook, less waiting by the hungry ones, savings in the cost of food and camp-stove fuel. No other camp kettle can make this statement!

If you're intrigued by pressure cooking, as I was, there's no reason why you can't borrow a cooker for a trial run, as I did. In the event the instruction booklet has been mislaid, I would suggest that you obtain another copy from the cooker's manufacturer or from a dealer. You won't need a stationary engineer's license to operate it. In fact, you need not be particularly hungry to enjoy its output!

Incidentally, none of the unkind outpourings I've made heretofore regarding aluminum apply in the case of pressure cookers. Aluminum is fine.

Chapter XIV

Cooking
With
Foil

MY SOLE objection to aluminum foil lies in its indestructibility. I can tear it, shred it, crumple it, stomp on it, but like an irresistible monster in a horror movie, it continues to glint back evilly, repulsive on the landscape, a constant reminder of the slovenly who won't trouble to seek out a trash barrel. Candy wrappers, cigarette packages, and even old undershirts rot and disintegrate in a season or two, disappearing into the deepening duff of the forest floor. But not aluminum foil! In hundreds of sacred precincts it leers at me from the shadow of Lady Slippers or peeps lewdly from under shy Indian Pipes. It lingers in campground fireplaces, impervious to flame. I suppose it's part of the "price we pay for progress." At any rate, I'm sure that future astronauts will have little trouble spotting the United States from 100,000 miles away. Their target will glow from coast to coast with littered aluminum foil!

Up to the ugly point of its indiscriminate disposal, however, aluminum foil is an unadulterated blessing to camp cooks. The uses to which it can be put form a list which the most assiduous writer couldn't keep up to date. Most are improvisations, the majority highly practical, although there persist borderline suggestions for useless makeshifts, such as the reflector oven made up of forked sticks and foil which, if anyone seriously attempted to build, would require an hour's work, and only a light breeze to tear it apart. Aluminum foil is not a magical material which has outmoded the frying pan or stew pot. It's simply a fine aid to camp cooking and, when held in that light, wonders of convenience can be accomplished with it. For example, it's easier to keep the interior of a camp stove clean if it's lined with foil. Instead of scrubbing away at grease accumulations and baked-on food bits, lifting out the foil liner removes them.

As already suggested, lining a rusted reflector oven with foil will increase its efficiency, and soot can be kept from the exterior of a campfire cook kettle by wrapping the outside.

While the cook-kit covers are busy pretending to be frying pans, kettle covers can be improvised with foil for speedier cooking. Lining the interior of a skillet when frying will save washing it. Too, a lining will prevent a "fishy" taste being imparted to the pan when fish are cooked. If more than one food is being prepared, raise the foil into a slight ridge to form a compartmented pan.

Foil can, of course, be shaped to form biscuit tins, cake pans, muffin or cupcake trays. You can even form an egg poacher to fit into a small saucepan. Theorists often suggest foil kettles, hanging from wire coat hangers or green sticks, but this too often results in converting the soup to a fire extinguisher!

A drip tray can be attached to a wire broiler to catch meat drippings, as I've already pointed out, and foods being cooked on a spit over an open fire won't scorch as easily or become sooty if wrapped in foil.

I shudder to suggest that dinnerware be lined with it to save on dishwashing, but it *is* practical. Or it can be used on the plate for the first course then removed to supply a clean plate for dessert—rather expensive neatness!

Some campgrounds are equipped with individual sunken ice chests whose interiors can be made more attractive for food storage when lined with foil, and as a guarantee that they'll be dry in an emergency, keep a few dozen wooden or kitchen matches wrapped in aluminum.

The effectiveness of a Coleman oven can be improved by partially covering the holes atop the oven. Where metal fireboxes are supplied instead of fireplaces, as in Minnesota state parks, lay foil atop the fire unit and cook such foods as hamburgers and frankfurts directly on it.

Heavy-duty foil, about twice the thickness of the regular grade, is best suited to camp cooking, and it makes little difference whether the satin or shiny side is next to the food. When lining a reflector oven, however, the shiny side will do a slightly better job of reflecting heat. Much foil cooking is done by wrapping and sealing foods so that no moisture escapes, thus preserving flavor, vitamins, and minerals much as with a pressure cooker. In wrapping foods which must be turned occasionally or which must be placed directly on hot coals, use a double wrapping of foil —not a single sheet doubled over, but two separate wrappings. If the outer foil should be punctured in handling, the inner layer still confines those precious juices. Also, to some degree, scorching is less likely. Generally, foods should be wrapped loosely. The best method is the so-called "drug-store wrap," whereby foil is folded over the food so that its edges meet. These are then folded together two or three times, thus effecting a complete seal. Don't simply roll food in the foil. This will allow the escape of moisture and flavor!

FOIL RECIPES

Probably the most common use for foil is in the baking of potatoes over a campfire or in its coals. Few apparently realize, however, that red hot coals alone are unsuitable for this. They should be mixed with hot ashes to temper the heat. Otherwise, potatoes acquire a heavy coating of unappetizing carbon!

Tasty Taters
Pare and cut into 6 pieces 1 potato for each member of the family. Sprinkle with dry onion soup mix, add 1 tablespoon water and a pat of butter. Seal in foil and bake in coals-and-ashes for about 25 minutes or for 30 to 40 minutes on fireplace grate over medium flames.

Cheesed Potatoes
Pare and slice 3 large potatoes on foil. Sprinkle with salt and pepper to suit. Crumple on 4 or 5 slices of crisp bacon. Add 1 large sliced onion and 2 cups of cubed American cheese. Slice one stick (½ cup) of margarine or

butter over all and mix on foil. Seal well in double wrap allowing space for steam expansion. Cook on fireplace grill for about 40 minutes. Makes six servings.

Butter-Baked Potatoes

Probably the simplest of baked potatoes. Scrub spuds well, rub skins heavily with butter, and wrap securely. Bacon grease may be substituted for butter for slightly different flavor. Will probably require 50 minutes on grill, 25 to 30 minutes in coals and ashes, depending upon size of potatoes and intensity of fire.

Candied Sweet Potatoes

Canned sweet potatoes will serve. Quarter potatoes lengthwise on foil, add 2 tablespoons water and sprinkle with about ½ cup brown sugar. Seal tightly, bake 20 minutes on grill, 10 minutes on each side.

Campfire Corn

Pull back husks and remove silk. Brush with margarine or butter, replace husks, wrap in foil, twisting each end to seal. Roast 15 to 20 minutes on fireplace grill. These should be turned occasionally. If time permits, soak one hour in water after removing silk and before buttering.

Mexican Maize

Cut kernels from cob with sharp knife onto sheet of foil. (Lacking fresh corn, canned whole kernel variety may be substituted). Add tomato, onion, and green pepper chopped together, plus dab of butter or margarine, and season to suit. Seal tightly and cook on fireplace grate 20 to 25 minutes.

Grilled Cabbage

For each serving make up aluminum package with 1 cup of chopped raw cabbage, salt and pepper, pat of butter, and 1 tablespoon of milk or cream, preferably the latter if available. Seal tightly and grill about 30 minutes.

Skinon Onions

Wash onion, leaving the skin on. Wrap by gathering

foil about the onion and twisting at the top. Cook on grill about 40 minutes, turning frequently. It's easy to tell when the onion is done; it's soft to the touch.

Vegetable Hoedown

For each serving, slice 1 fresh tomato, add 1 slice of onion, sliced mushroom (or buttons), 1 tablespoon green peas, 1 tablespoon diced carrots, and a pat of margarine or butter. Season well, wrap tightly, and cook on fireplace grill 30 minutes.

Cohasset Carrots

Wash and scrub 2 carrots per serving. Lay these side by side on foil (don't stack them one atop the other when wrapping) and butter generously. Seal tightly and grill on fireplace 35 to 40 minutes.

Peas and Rice

Mix one small can of peas with double the amount of cooked instant rice, including a small amount of the pea liquid. Add a large pat of butter or margarine, salt and pepper. Seal and cook 10 to 15 minutes.

Megunticook Meat Loaf

To 1 pound of ground meat, add ½ cup of bread crumbs, ½ cup barbecue sauce (use 2 tablespoons catsup if sauce is not available), ½ small chopped onion, ¼ chopped green pepper. Mix well, wrap in foil and bake in coals-and-ashes for about an hour, turning every 15 minutes. Meat loaf will stick to foil slightly, but the crunchy scrapings are tasty! Serves four.

Simple Hamburgers

Wrap ground meat patty with 1 or 2 slices of onion and a pat of butter or margarine. Seal tightly. For medium-done, cook on fireplace grill about 10 minutes, turning once.

Liver Burgers

Make a "sandwich" of two thin hamburger patties with a thin slice of liverwurst (dabbed with prepared mustard) between. Wrap tightly and cook for 10 to 15 minutes, turning several times. Serve on buns or with potatoes and Vegetable Hoedown.

Lumberjack Franks
Cut frankfurts lengthwise but not all the way through. Stuff with a simple bread dressing or chopped onion and pickle relish mixture. Wrap each frank in one slice of bacon, seal individually, and cook on grill 8 to 10 minutes. Turn occasionally.

Aroostook Pork Chop
Place thin slices potato atop single pork chop from which fat has *not* been trimmed. Seal tightly in double wrap and cook on grill 20 minutes on "potato side," 10 minutes more on other.

Sausage Cortland
On sausage patty place ¼-inch thick slice apple sprinkled with brown sugar and a dash of cinnamon. Wrap tightly and cook 20 minutes on grill. If only link sausage is available, precook in ½-inch of water to draw off excess grease. Alternate links with thin quarters of apple. Sprinkle and cook as above.

Ham
Spread both sides of one slice of ham with prepared mustard and sprinkle with brown sugar. Lay this in foil between bits of pineapple. Add a little juice, too. Seal tightly and cook atop grill about 45 minutes or until ham is done.

Foiled Fish
Someone in camp caught a mess of half-pound trout (or any other small fish, for that matter). Clean, wash, and scale if necessary (trout don't need it). Lay fish on foil atop one slice of bacon, bunch thinly sliced potato and chopped onion about it, add another slice of bacon atop fish. Seal individual servings tightly in double thickness and broil on coals about 10 minutes.

Hidden Biscuits

Grease foil almost to edges and wrap gobs of biscuit dough loosely to allow for rising. Place tightly sealed package on fireplace grill, turning it once halfway through recommended baking time for biscuits.

Hot French Bread

Slash loaf of French bread on the bias in 1-inch slices, being careful not to cut through bottom crust. Mix soft butter with either onion salt or garlic powder. Spread on one side of each slice. Wrap double and heat on grill 20 to 30 minutes, turning occasionally.

Note: Cooking times are all approximate and must vary according to size of portions, intensity of fire, quality of hardwood coals, and whether meals are prepared atop fireplace grill or in coals. This means there's an element of gambling in foil cooking—at least until experience transforms it into a more exact science. However, since well-sealed foil prevents the escape of moisture, serious scorching is infrequent.

Chapter XV

Indian
Style

MOST CAMPERS tote a spade solely for ditching a tent. Certainly, few have in mind bean-hole beans or a New England clambake. It's not that campers particularly shun the companionship of a shovel. It's just that, as far as the unknowing are concerned, anything cooked underground must certainly be gritty with gravel. Such nonsense is not for them.

Maybe it's just as well. If all campers realized the ease with which pit cooking can be accomplished and the succulency of the product, America would become pockmarked from Skowhegan to Spokane with steaming pits from which would drift aromas of baked beans, steamed lobsters, baked pike, and roast haunches. As it is, only the adventuresome get to relish the delights of cooking "Indian style." It's a small select group—one that goes quietly about its digging, cooking, and smacking of lips.

Of course, there's nothing new about cooking in the ground. Indians made frequent pilgrimages to salt water where they held seafood festivals long before the first Viking sail was sighted. At Damariscotta, Maine, there still exists a giant prehistoric shell heap which attests eloquently to the frequency and scope of these early clambakes.

Granted, pit cooking is not possible during all camping trips. Many campgrounds forbid digging and, even where permissible, a one-or-two-day stop hardly warrants the effort involved. However, for those campers who "stay put" for some time, pit cooking offers the camp cook a chance to express himself in the ultimate medium.

BEAN-HOLE BEANS

The bean-hole is probably an outgrowth of the early Indian pit, since the principle involved is much the same. Directions for building a bean-hole vary, usually according to its proposed capacity. It's just as easy to bake a large pot of beans as a small one and, as with a good stew, each warming improves the batch. So I use a 12-inch cast-iron Dutch oven with a capacity of 4 pounds of dried beans, enough for some 20 servings. To accommodate this large kettle, I've maintained two permanent pits 3 feet deep and roughly 30 inches in diameter at the top, tapering to some 16 inches at the bottom.

The bottom and the sides are lined with field stone. For a permanent bean hole, the rocks are a necessity to keep the walls from crumbling and, too, they aid greatly in retaining heat. However, for a temporary pit, the rocks may be omitted and the hole dug proportionally smaller. It should be large enough so that about 6 inches of coals surround the pot and deep enough so that 12 to 14 inches of soil covers it. The pot need not be cast iron. An old-fashioned earthenware pot, such as grandmother used in her black-iron kitchen range, is excellent and may still be found in country stores, if not in the attic. It's even possible to use a cook-kit kettle.

Building the fire in the pit is no more difficult than atop the ground and, surprisingly, you'll have little trouble with lack of draft. Use ample tinder and dry softwood kindling, adding hardwood (split no thicker than 3 inches), as the blaze gets under way briskly. Any of the long-burning, coal-producing hardwoods are excellent. Keep the fire going until you have about 12 inches of live coals, a 1- to 2-hour chore.

The dried beans should be "put to soak" overnight in a kettle no more than ⅞ full and with at least 3 inches of water covering the beans. Otherwise, you may find that some of them have climbed over the side during the night! My favorites are California or Michigan pea beans or, if I'm planning to make a chile con carne with the "warmovers," I use red kidneys. Equally delectable are yellow eyes, soldier, or navy beans. Be sure to cull them of impurities such as tiny stones.

While the bean hole is "firing-up" simmer the soaked beans in fresh water until the skins crack and begin to curl, usually about 45 minutes. Don't boil them vigorously or you'll lose flavor. Some cooks add a teaspoon of soda during simmering, as any New Englander will straight-facedly tell you, "to remove the snappers"—probably about as effective as putting on bed slippers to kick the cussedness out of a bobcat! With or without soda, pour off the water after simmering.

Recipes vary greatly and even these need not be followed to the letter. In fact, when it comes to stirring up a touse, religion and politics are as bland as a discussion of a PTA cooky sale compared to an exchange of views on bean-baking recipes! I know two Down East maiden ladies who haven't spoken to each other for nine years because one of them casually remarked to a friend that "Ethel's pea beans are a mite mollasy." Whether or not Ethel likes it, these are the ingredients I prefer, proportioned for a 2-pound (dried) batch:

½ pound salt pork
1 large onion
¾ cup molasses
3 tablespoons brown sugar
1 teaspoon dry mustard
1 teaspoon salt

Mix the molasses, brown sugar, salt, and mustard in 1 to 1½ cups of hot water, stirring well until the salt and sugar are dissolved. The above proportions, of course, may be varied to suit individual tastes. In fact, when I worked in lumbercamps in northern Maine, the cooks prepared two batches of beans—twice a week—one with molasses for the Yankee lumberjacks and one without for the predominantly French-Canadian choppers. There were onions in both, however. There are those, too, who will suggest catsup for a bit of tomato taste, a topic upon which I would prefer not to comment!

In the bottom of the bean pot, lay one to three slices of salt pork (the fatter the better) ⅜ to ½-inch thick. Next, add a layer of beans, 2 to 4 inches deep. Over these, place onion slices and more salt pork , then more beans, building up the layers until the pot is full. If you're a showman and expect observers at "the opening," arrange the final layer of onions and pork in an artistic manner on top. Pour in the molasses-and-brown-sugar syrup and add hot water to just below the level of the beans. Put on the cover and hie yourself to the bean hole.

Here, remove all but 6 to 8 inches of the coals, placing the pot atop those remaining in the hole. Pack more coals around the pot but not on top of it. Unless the cover fits snugly, it's wise to drape this with aluminum foil to prevent dirt from slipping into the pot. Place a layer of sod or wet burlap over it and fill the hole. Note the time and 6 to 8 hours later, excavate carefully.

The preliminary digging I will trust to almost anyone, but as the spade approaches the precious vessel, I prefer to take over. I want no careless oaf prying open the lid to admit gravel and ashes. Once the bail appears above the soil, grasp this firmly and heave upward. It will be hot! A pot holder or asbestos glove may be used as protection to the hand, of course, but this is crassly prosaic. I much prefer a forked stick cut from a rugged young maple. Place the pot on the ground and carefully brush away all coals and ashes from the cover. The baker-of-beans' moment of truth is not unlike that of the bull fighter. There's no turning back at this moment and there can be no hesitancy. Opening a bean hole calls for showmanship and stage presence. Lift the lid confidently and with just a bit of a flourish. Failures are rare. Chances are that, as the beans are unveiled, your audience will be moved to huzzahs at the sight. The beans will be a shade of brown unknown except in a bean pot (Who ever heard of a bean-brown barn, for example?) and the gold of the onions will blend subtly with that of the pork. The aroma? Only a Hemingway can describe it. The flavor? That's the reason my kettle is large!

THE NEW ENGLAND CLAMBAKE

In a sense, "New England Clambake" is a misnomer. It's not confined to New England, by any means. Seafoods are cooked similarly anywhere along our seacoasts. The main course is not necessarily clams—in fact, particularly in Maine, lobster is more likely to form the pièce de résistance with clams, sweet corn, potatoes, and frankfurters appearing as supplements. Some cooks include chicken, but this is not at its best when steamed unless it is also broiled to a golden brown just before eating. Finally, as a sort of coup de grâce to the term, the food is not baked. It is steamed. Call it what you may, however, it's in New England, and particularly on the Maine coast, that the clambake reaches culinary heights, although Massachusetts, Rhode Island, and Connecticut might dispute the claim and probably with some justification.

Oceanside campgrounds are growing in number and popularity, the delights of campfire-cooked seafoods undoubtedly contributing to this. Fortunately, the locale for a clambake is usually "good diggin'," since it's likely to be on a shady beach or among sand dunes just out of reach of the pounding surf. The technique calls for a pit, easier to prepare than a bean hole with its width and depth governed by the extent of the proposed menu. For the average family, a pit 2 feet wide, 3 feet long, and some 16 inches deep, is probably handiest. The bottom should be lined with rocks, with one tier along the sidewalls. Some New Englanders protest that only "round rocks" are fitting, but I can't understand why oblong, rectangular, square, or just plain rocks aren't as suitable. One point to keep in mind, however: Rocks that have been lying in the water may explode when heated. Choose those above the high tide mark.

A fire is built in the pit—of driftwood, of course. Fill the pit with fire and keep it blazing until the rocks are white hot. The advice from one "expert" suggests that rocks be "red hot," but I doubt that he ever tried to bake a piece of the Maine coast! Some "clambakers" mix rocks with firewood so that these heat more quickly and then settle to the bottom of the pit as the fire dies down. When the fire is finished, remove any unburned or smoldering sticks, then lay 6 to 8 inches of seaweed directly atop the glowing coals.

While the fire is heating the pit stones, prepare the food for cooking. If clams are to be included these should be scrubbed to eliminate all sand which might cling to them. Rinse them in water several times. To aid in loosening clinging grit, add a handful of corn meal to the water. Silk should be removed from sweet corn, but not the husks. For added tangy flavor, don't wrap corn in foil. Potatoes and onions should be washed but not peeled. Frankfurts may be wrapped in foil and chicken is best cut into breast, wing, and leg pieces. Lobster needs no special preparation except to make certain that it is alive when placed in the pit. Never cook and eat lobster that is not obviously frisky.

Generally, three layers of food are placed in the pit, with a layer of seaweed 4 to 8 inches thick between each. First the clams go in on the bottom strata of seaweed. The next food layer consists entirely of lobster while the top layer may be made up of any combination of corn, potatoes, sausage (wrapped in foil), frankfurts (also wrapped), onions, and chicken. The entire assortment is then covered with a final layer of 6 to 8 inches of seaweed overlaid with a tarpaulin or wet burlap. The edges should be fastened down against a sea breeze and sand piled on top. Cook some 1 to 1½ hours, the exact time depending on the intensity of the heat in the stones, the amount of food, and how well sealed the pit is. To test the food, open the nearest lobster. Its meat should be white, flaky, and slightly tinged with red.

A nutcracker is the handiest tool for cracking lobster shells and an old-fashioned two-tined fork aids in picking out the meat. Dip both clams and lobster bits in drawn butter before eating. Mustard and relishes for the hot dogs, and butter for the corn and potatoes embellish the salt-water flavor.

Proper attire for the occasion is important. Sneakers which may be tossed into a laundromat washer, old dungarees, and rolled-up sleeves are in order. A large bib is the only concession to gentility. Eating is done with the fingers and only the unacquainted ask for napkins, knife, or spoon. When the pit is empty, a nap on the beach is indicated with the rumble of surf as a lullaby, although some of the rumble may be gastronomical. If you get washed out to sea at high tide, don't fret. It's a beautiful way to go!

A KETTLE CLAMBAKE

A more orderly and tidier New Englander favors the kettle clambake. There, seaweed lines the bottom of a large kettle and one lobster per person is laid upon this. These, in turn, are covered with more seaweed, then a layer of sweet corn, more seaweed, and, finally, clams. These are topped with seaweed and the kettle covered and placed over a fire to cook for 1 to 1½ hours. The clams are eaten first, and when these are gone, the corn will be ready. This disposed of, the lobster awaits on the bottom layer. Personally, I prefer to get to the bottom of things, bypassing the clams and corn!

This is not, of course, a form of pit cooking but it deviates only slightly and offers a more direct route to the same toothsome flavor.

Chapter XVI

Sourdough
Cooking

SOURDOUGH, to most, is an 1898 Alaskan miner who mushed across frozen wastes by day and spent his nights waltzing dance-hall girls around under the steely eye of the Royal Canadian Mounted Police—any one of whom, incidentally, could recite "The Cremation of Sam McGee" or get his man with equal ease. The definition is probably as accurate as any, except that it fails to point out that sourdough was also an agent for leavening breads and hot cakes.

Baking soda or "saleratus" was known in the North, but a steady diet of foods containing it led to indigestion and heartburn. Baking powder, when first introduced, found little acceptance among the veterans of Chilkoot Pass and other parts of the North. In fact, baking powder was accorded short shrift. The stuff, it seems, was believed to have the power to curtail a man's virility to the point where a Saturday night in town was hardly worth the trouble!

Hence, every miner kept, on the back of the stove, a "starter pot," usually of earthenware or simply a crude wooden bowl made from a "junk" of birch. A tin lard pail might do temporarily but this was likely to rust through quickly. Into this went a concoction made up of flour, salt, sugar, and a bit of water, all kept warm so that it fermented and gave off an odor which might well send a Chee-chako reeling toward the door and fresh air! Whenever some of the "starter" was taken from the pot for pancakes or biscuits, it was replenished by the addition of a little more flour and water so that, according to some historians, some starters were reportedly fifty or more years old—and still in use! Such reports are probably as accurate as the woodsman's claim for his ancient axe: She's twelve years old," he boasted. "Had three new heads 'n' seven new handles!"

The Alaskan Sourdough didn't invent his namesake. No one knows how long before Christ it was in use, although some attribute its discovery to Egyptians about 4,000 B.C. Sourdough was in use among American pioneers. In early New England, it took the forms of "leavins," kept on the back shelf of the stove or near the fireplace. Sourdough went West and rode chuckwagons on cattle drives before going on to join the Gold Rush of '98.

Sourdough cooking still has its appeal and it is apparently making a comeback, probably for the same reason that run-down colonial houses are being restored and rebuilt Model T's chug once more on our roads. Eating sourdough pancakes, however, is decidedly more fun than trying to plumb a 1754 outhouse or risking life and limb in a cantankerous Lizzie. You have only to wade through a batch, slobbered with farm butter and dripping with maple syrup, to be convinced.

The sourdough of the Alaskan or Yukon miner didn't travel well since it had to be kept warm. Therefore, it was generally used only within a cabin. It did occasionally make a trip on a river barge or even on a pack mule. When one such mule went over a cliff, the miner scrambled down to the dead animal and scraped the remains of his sourdough from the poor critter's face into a tobacco can. A sourdough starter was that hard to come by! We now know, however, that sourdough can be refrigerated without damage except to slow, temporarily, its fermenting. A potent liquid may form on top, but this may be stirred back in. Some Alaskan coastal Indians didn't stir it back in. They skimmed it off and drank it, thereby developing the original lost weekend and the biggest hangover south of Nome!

Today's sourdough can travel harmlessly aboard a station wagon, along with a camper's other gear. The top of an earthenware pot, for example, can be sealed with masking tape to prevent spilling en route. In fact, there are available special "starter pots" with tightly fitting covers! Incidentally, keep the cover on at all times, but especially at night. At Kamankeag Pond, Maine, one morning, I found a dead mouse in mine. It was probably overcome by the fumes and fell in.

A "starter" can be made almost anywhere but probably most conveniently at home, prior to a camping trip. Into the pot put 4 cups of flour, 1 teaspoon of salt, 4 tablespoons of sugar, and 3 to 4 cups of lukewarm water. Stir this until it forms a smooth paste with a consistency not unlike that of thin pancake batter. The warming shelf of the old-time kitchen range was the best spot in which to keep the pot, but since this has passed into museums, almost any area will do that has a comfortable room temperature of 68 to 72 degrees.

The mixture will take four to five days to sour during which it should be stirred frequently and gently. When ready for use, the culture should have a bubbly appearance and a definitely sour smell, though this will not be as objectionable as I may have implied! Souring can be hastened by adding a little dry yeast or vinegar, in which case it will take about three days. However, yeast or vinegar are not cricket if you want the authentic stuff!

If the starter is not to be used for some time, souring may be overdone and its odor may be slightly overpronounced. The pot then needs "freshening." To accomplish this, add one cup of warm water and one cup of flour to each cup of starter and mix well, stirring gently again and never beating. When thoroughly blended, discard all but an amount equal to that originally in the pot.

Sourdough Pancakes

Like baked beans, sourdough pancakes require preparation the night before, although this will entail only a few minutes. To your sourdough pot add 2 cups of flour, 1½ tablespoons of sugar, and a husky pinch of salt, plus about 2 cups of tepid water. Blend this gently. I can't overstress the gentle treatment required! You'll find that the sourdough consistency has thickened somewhat but this will thin down during the night. Keep the pot warm.

Breakfast preparation then entails pouring out all but 1

to 2 cups of the sourdough into a mixing bowl. Blend in 2 tablespoons of sugar, 3 tablespoons of butter, and an egg, stirring thoroughly and—once again—gently! And now, for an old Alaskan's secret: Dissolve 1 teaspoon of soda into about ⅓ cup of boiling water. Then fold the soda mixture into the batter slowly, working the mixing spoon throughout the bowl. You will then see *and hear* the batter going into action, displaying a frothy-like behavior!

Sourdough pancakes require a hot griddle or skillet. Grease this lightly, preferably by rubbing it with a bacon rind, although lumber-camp cooks often prefer a piece of salt pork from which the salty crustiness has been washed. Sourdough pancakes should not be the size of cartwheels. Popular illustrations invariably show flapjacks the size of a Frenchman's beret being tossed into the air. Nonsense! They shouldn't be tossed; neither should they be much larger than a Model A hubcap! Old sourdoughs, in fact, maintained that one mixing spoonful of batter was enough for one pancake! When its top surface begins to bubble, or resemble the surface of the moon, and its edges begin to crust a little, it's time to turn the pancake over, once! And, once only. Only a tenderfoot cook flips them over repeatedly.

It takes a dedicated cook to serve up pancakes properly, since they should be served directly from the skillet or griddle—not piled in a warming oven to keep warm until everyone can eat together. Stacked on a plate they'll grow heavy and soggy. Serve with plenty of butter, syrup, honey, or jam. The cook can get his later!

What do sourdough pancakes taste like? Certainly nothing like their name implies. Ambrosia is the favorite, if overworked, term applied to them by Alaskans, but how can even the most thoroughly schooled Sourdough transform a flavor into a sentence? You'll be convinced only when you've tried them!

Sourdough Biscuits

1 cup sourdough	2 teaspoons baking powder
⅓ cup cold water	1 husky pinch salt
2 cups flour	1 similarly husky pinch soda
½ cup butter, margarine, or shortening	

Mix the baking powder, flour, salt, and soda. Blend in melted shortening, butter, or margarine, then add sourdough and cold water. Mix this well until a heavy, slightly sticky dough results. Whether you're using a Dutch oven or a biscuit sheet for other types of ovens, "pinch off" gobs of dough one and a half times the size of a golf ball. In a Coleman oven, bake at 425 to 450 degrees until done—probably a matter of 10 to 15 minutes. For reflector oven baking, place close to a brisk fire until the biscuits rise, being careful not to scorch the front edges. Then set the oven back slightly until they're done. In a Dutch oven, biscuits are often best baked in a pie tin set atop a trivet in the oven. This prevents scorching on the bottom should the underneath coals get overenthusiastic in their work.

Sourdough Muffins

1 cup sourdough	1 egg
2 cups flour	2 tablespoons shortening
½ cup sugar	½ teaspoon baking soda
½ cup milk	

Mix all ingredients well, adding the sourdough last, so that it forms a thick but "runny" batter. Stir rather than beat. Fill muffin-tin cups about half full and bake for 30 minutes, or until done, in a Coleman oven at 375 degrees. For reflector or Dutch oven baking, follow the same directions given for biscuits. For a toothsome deviation, add a cup of strained blueberries or raisins. Surprisingly, even whole kernel corn makes a nice additive!

So much for simple sourdough recipes. But how about the care and cultivation of the starter? Never use the entire contents of your sourdough pot. Always leave at least one cup of culture. Many advise that replenishing is simply a matter of adding flour and water, but rarely is anyone specific on this point! Some unknowing ones even suggest the further addition of sugar or salt, probably the same who insist that clam chowder needs tomatoes!

Proper care of the starter culture calls for scraping the sides of the pot and dissolving these scrapings into the contents, adding tepid water, to form a thin paste. Then add flour and stir until your arm cries out in pain. Put the cover back on and "let 'er set." Never return to the starter pot any batter containing ingredients other than flour or water. Particularly avoid eggs. On cold nights, I've known sourdough addicts to wrap the starter pot in a blanket—the camping equipment industry not yet having come up with a sleeping bag for a sourdough crock!

Sourdough cooking is not for every camper. It entails somewhat more trouble than ripping open a package mix. However, today's Sourdough drives a station wagon, not a mule, and I suspect that he secretly holds in disdain those who dream up those beautiful instant cakes!

Chapter XVII

Dehydrated
Foods

ELEANOR has never forgiven a New York outfitter for the frustrating hours we spent, some twenty-five years ago while on a two-week canoe trip, trying unsuccessfully to cook and eat dehydrated foods he'd sold us. We'd failed to mash the potatoes, even with an axe; the eggs had valiantly resisted being eaten and had won; the vegetables, Eleanor swore, had been plaster-of-Paris display samples. Personally, I disagree with my wife. The stuff was war surplus—grapeshot left over from the War of 1812!

Modern processing has cleansed my thoughts regarding the stufff, but Eleanor still generates unladylike thinking concerning it. Most women feel the same way. Yet they'll come home from the supermarket laden down with instant mashed or scalloped potatoes, grated cheese, dried soups, quick gravies, minute frostings, and presto sauces—all of which have been subjected to complete or partial dehydration. I've pointed this out, only to be assailed by the typical female logic that "these are different," and I know better than to pursue the matter. The fact is, supermarket shelves are piled high with various dehydrated foods ideally suited to camping.

The word "dehydrated" is a nasty one and food processors have given it a wide berth. Instead they use "instant," "quick," or "minute."

A quick trip among supermarket shelves will reveal dozens of such foods, although none will bear the odious label "dehydrated." They are, nevertheless, just that.

Dehydrated foods have been with us a long time. The

Indians, particularly Western tribes, used a form of dehydration when they made jerky, a lean meat, sliced thin and dried in the sun on a rack over a smoky fire which aided the drying and which kept away blowflies. Pemmican, made from jerky, became a trail food that lasted almost indefinitely without refrigeration. Earlier forms of dehydration by white men consisted of heating, but not cooking, foods, and this process was marked by a notable loss of flavor.

The latest process is known as "freeze-drying," developed by the drug industry for preserving certain pharmaceuticals. Food packers have adapted it to produce camping meals that are lightweight, easily prepared, and surprisingly palatable. Fresh or cooked foods are quick-frozen and then placed in a vacuum cabinet wherein air pressure is reduced to one millimeter or approximately 1/800th of normal. Heat is then applied in such a manner that ice crystals in the food are directly transformed to vapor. As a result, salts, sugars, and proteins are dried within the foods with about 98 percent of the moisture removed. This eliminates the later need for refrigeration and minimizes shrinkage or shriveling without affecting nutritional value or palatability. Rehydration requires only minutes.

The process is still limited, however. Armour, for example, which pioneered in the freeze-drying of foods, found that best results were obtained with cuts of meat less than one inch thick. Larger cuts take too long to process to be practical and that's why beef or pork roasts are not available. Practically every other type of meal is, though!

During the spring of 1963 I decided to combine the opening of my camp with an experiment in freeze-dried living. One of the large packers supplied some three cases of freeze-dried "complete meals" and, in addition, I stocked up on orange juice crystals, powdered soups, dehydrated coffee cream, and instant puddings, none of which required refrigeration. I included no fresh foods, no canned goods. I lived on the stuff for a week during which I wrestled with a chain saw, patched leaky roofs, repaired washed-out roads, and cleaned up blowdowns. If dehydrated and freeze-dried foods could keep me happy under these conditions, I figured Eleanor might, at long last, grant forgiveness!

None of the meals took over 40 minutes to prepare, and most of them less than 30. Once cooked, the meals had eye appeal. Scrambled eggs looked like eggs and they'd lost their latex consistency. Flavor was good. Pork chops were golden brown, tasty, but somewhat tough. The stews, chicken and beef, were delicious. The only outright failure was beefsteak, which was tough *and* tasteless. I lost four pounds during the week, but I think the chain saw gnawed this away, not my diet.

The flavor of freeze-dried foods won't make grandmother cry herself to sleep with a broken heart. It falls short of good home cooking and is no match for the masterpieces of the better eating houses. But it *is* tastier, by far, than some of the "chef's specials" I've had slung at me in roadside restaurants and in many a super-highway service-plaza hash house!

The savings in weight, although not a critical factor for family campers, are, nevertheless, just a little astounding. A 32-ounce beef stew, for example, weighs a mere 6 ounces before preparation. A Swiss steak dinner, weighing better than 2 pounds on the table, is a trifling 7 ounces in its aluminum-lined packet. Four pork chops, minus bone and excess fat, weigh in at 3 ounces!

I'm a lover of country sausage and pork chops, but these keep in camp about as well as a keg of cold beer at a firemen's picnic. Freeze-drying, however, makes them possible even for extended trips without refrigeration. Flavor is a bit shy of the real thing, true, but not enough so that it spoils a meal a hundred miles back in the bush!

Preparation has been simplified so that getting meals is as easy, and in some cases, easier than preparing fresh or canned foods. Most ingredients are rehydrated by soaking in water for up to 10 minutes. Some require a short period of simmering. In many instances, particularly in the case of stews, cooking has already been done. It's then simply a matter of rehydrating and heating thoroughly. I discovered that scrambled eggs could be prepared by adding a bit of hot water to the packet, shaking, seasoning, and eating!

Understandably, these foods are the mainstay of hikers, mountain climbers, and canoeists. I wish they'd been available when I worked as a forest fire lookout in New Hampshire years ago when every ounce of food, including canned goods, had to be toted up the mountain on foot. I recall that I climbed a total of 153,932 feet that summer, and I ain't clum a mountain since!

Any advertising that proclaims the *necessity* of freeze-dried or dehydrated foods for family campers must, at best, have a pronounced limp. Family campers are rarely more than 15 minutes from a store and modern station wagons merely squat a little lower when a hundred pounds of canned goods and fresh goodies are piled on the roof rack or tailgate.

Nevertheless, these modern food wonders have a place in family camping. It's fun to prepare in 40 minutes a beef stew that might otherwise require at least 2 hours. Mom may well appreciate this convenience when she arrives in camp all played out after having climbed up to Indian Leap! Occasionally, too, you may be caught short on a Sunday when country stores are closed. Too, the foods are a good change-of-pace novelty. They're work savers. I keep a half-dozen packages of assorted full meals in our camp kit at all times. Strangely, they're not available in food stores. Most are marketed through sporting-goods and camping-equipment dealers.

Freeze-dried foods, especially, and some dehydrated versions, will cost you more than will supermarket meals for the same reason it's more costly to fly from New York to Los Angeles than it is to go by bus. Waste has been eliminated. Vegetables have been sorted, trimmed, cleaned, and cooked. Meats have been boned and excess fat removed. Refrigeration is unnecessary. Shelf life is guaranteed from one to two years. All of these conveniences cost money.

Low daily costs for feeding families are repeatedly cited in advertising. Choosing from among the offerings of several firms, I came up with the figure of $1.83 per day per person. Most economical for family groups are the beef and chicken stews. Most expensive are eggs, which approximate $3.25 a dozen! Such cost appraisals, however, are not complete. Freeze-dried foods don't satisfy the craving for certain fresh foods. For example, there's no substitute for sweet corn fresh from the farmer's roadside stand, tomatoes still warm from the garden sun, or peas ripened on July 4th. Families with children, too, will want butter, jams, jellies, milk. The cost of these foods must, then, be added to those of the freeze-dried meals to get an accurate daily tabulation.

The sizes of portions, too, are often misrepresented. Full-meal packages labeled "Four Portions" may leave four adults looking around for more!

It has little bearing on the feasibility of dehydrated and freeze-dried foods for campers, but the gray-flannel suit clan has capitalized nauseously on man's fear, in order to peddle the stuff. One firm drags in Bible quotations! " . . . and there shall be famines, and pestilences, and earthquakes in divers places . . ." (Matthew 24:7)—justifies the outfit's claim that every family should have a year's supply on hand in case the Big Bomb goes Boom.

Another noxious ad offers a 72-hour emergency kit for a family of six. In fine print, leering from its bilious pages, is the suggestion that one person can live on this kit for twenty-one days. No doubt there's a stiletto hidden in the pea soup powder with which that "one person" can do in the other five, thus gaining for himself an additional eighteen days! Another folder illustrates the chaos of crumbling buildings, a mushroom cloud in the background, and crowds panicking in all directions. "It's too late to shop, now," says the caption. I'd eat braised moose hocks before buying these firms' offerings! These foods should be for good meals under blue skies and tall pines.

Packaging varies, of course, among the various firms, but generally, packets are available for 2, 4, 6, or 8 persons. Many offer complete menus, including breakfast, lunch, and dinner packets for a varying number of persons. Ingredients are usually contained in aluminum-lined heavy paper envelopes. Incidentally, during my week of dehydrated foods, I exposed several packages to the curiosity of mice, red squirrels, and even a weasel. All found the offerings uninteresting and none even nibbled at the sealed envelopes.

134

There is an amazing variety of available freeze-dried and dehydrated foods, both individual ingredients and full meals, designed primarily for campers. They include everything from applesauce mix, through "ranch-style breakfast and banana crystals."

Chapter XVIII

Game

Fish

Cooking

PRAISES BE, there are still youngsters who want to go fishing. They haven't *all* been regimented into little league baseball! Practically every family has one child who, prior to a camping trip, has pressured Pop into buying him an outfit. Not that this interest in angling is taken very seriously, for the outfit too often consists of a discount house bargain, hardly fit for use at the fish pond concession of a church fair. Pop, who probably spends 5 dollars a week bowling with the boys, figures the $2.97 rod, reel, and line "is good enough until we see if he likes fishing." Such a handicap doesn't phase most twelve-year-old boys!

However, what happens to a bluegill or to a solitary trout heralded by cries of "Hey, Mom! Hey, Dad! I got one" and which is triumphantly whisked into camp on a dead run? Too often, it's allowed to shrivel in the sun because no one wants to eat "the slimy thing," or more likely, the subject is artfully bypassed because no one is sure about cleaning procedure. Besides, how does one cook a fish that didn't come from the frozen food compartment at the supermarket? The boy's triumph fades with the fish's coloring and that's that!

This isn't the place for a discussion of fishing tackle or for a treatise on father-and-son relationships, except to point out that fishing with a shoddy outfit is no different from playing golf with a set of 19-dollar clubs. The handicap is almost insurmountable! Cheap fishing gear is practically worthless; whether it's to be used by a youngster or an adult, seek the advice of an experienced angler and buy according to his suggestions.

Because the bluegill is small, doesn't mean that it's unfit to eat. It's probably a far tastier morsel than the so-called "fresh fish" which has taken 12 to 48 hours to reach the supermarket refrigerator case. Freshly caught fish of almost any species is a delicacy. It's not difficult to learn to recognize the various fishes—there are dozens of well-illustrated and inexpensive manuals on the market. And fish is easy to cook.

Fish that are likely to be caught by family camping youngsters are usually the fresh-water species, including trout, bass, wall-eyed pike, pickerel, perch, catfish, horn pout, and the sunfishes: crappies, bluegills, and calico bass. Adult campers, who've acquired a little more angling skill and are apt to travel more extensively in search of good fishing, may well tie into and land such fish as salmon, muskellunge, lake trout, northern pike—all from fresh water, plus some of the ocean species like striped bass or shad.

Few realize—and this needn't complicate anyone's outlook on catch-it-yourself delicacies—that certain species have lean flesh and these include most of the fresh-water species except whitefish, catfish, horn pout, lake trout, and salmon. These are considered "fat" fish since their flesh tends to be somewhat more oily. Then, there are the so-called "scaleless" species, notably trout and salmon. Actually, these do have scales, but a trout's are so small they can be disregarded, while only larger salmon (two pounds or more) may require scaling. Such species as perch, pickerel, or bass should be scaled or skinned. Horn pout and catfish (they're closely related) definitely should be skinned. Of course, it's fun to catch the "big ones," but you'll find that their flavor falls far short of the taste of the more easily caught smaller fish. Large trout, for example, especially if they've been in warmer-than-usual water, will have a "muddy" taste. The best trout are those that will cause a game warden to haul out his tape measure! The apparent intricacy of fish characteristics may seem puzzling at first, but you'll soon untangle them, especially if you specialize in certain species, as most fishermen do.

Cleaning a fish is not nearly as distasteful a chore as some might imagine. To best preserve its flavor, it should be cleaned as soon as it is caught, but I've never known a fisherman to put aside his rod "when they're bitin'." However, clean them as soon as possible. A wet fish is difficult to hold; so grasp it with a paper towel or a handful of dry moss or grass. You'll need a sharp knife, the sharper, the better. Insert the point into the anal vent and run the blade up to the throat. Cut off the head immediately back of the gills and the tail far enough back to save as much of the meat as possible. The fins may or may not be removed. It's unimportant. The stomach cavity can now be opened and its contents pulled out easily. With your thumbnail, scrape away the blood along the backbone. Rinse the fish thoroughly in fresh water. Give no heed to those who proclaim that water should never touch a cleaned fish. That's nonsense! How else can you clean it well? However, once cleaned, wipe it dry inside and out.

Time and time again, I've seen the suggestion that a fishing creel be lined with grass. Don't do it! At least, not *green* grass. If fish are to be carried in a creel during the day, bed them in *dried* grass or moss. Green grass has a faint warmth that does them no good!

Even after it's placed in cold storage, fish should be accorded certain respect to hold it in flavorsome readiness for the skillet. Don't keep it in a pan of water! Nothing will make fish flesh soggier than water. Be careful, for example, that the drain plug in the camp ice chest is open, lest melting ice water reach the fish. Place it in the chest so that it cannot possibly get wet.

While a gourmet may go berserk with a wine bottle in cooking fish, most methods are simple and quick. There's no place for Trout Amandine in camp. You'll have a choice between broiling, frying, deep-frying, baking, or—and I use the term loosely—boiling.

Broiling, of all the methods, is kindest to flavor, and it's entirely practical in camp with fish weighing from ½ pound up to about 2 pounds. A fish larger than this should be filleted before broiling. To fillet, cut crosswise into the fish just back of the gill until the knife edge touches the backbone. Turn the blade flat with its edge facing toward the tail. Now slice along the spine until the knife edge emerges at the tail. It's that simple. Another method of preparing a larger fish for broiling is to slit the flesh down the back instead of along its belly when cleaning it. Then cut around the spine until the stomach cavity is reached. The fish can now be opened with its belly flesh acting as a "hinge."

Whether you use a vertical broiler or a horizontal grill, it should be greased to prevent the skin from sticking to it. During broiling, always baste or brush the fish with bacon, salt pork fat, or butter. Cooking oils help browning but contribute little to flavor. As I pointed out in Chapter IX, I prefer to do all broiling with food in a vertical position, but I'm not hard-nosed about it. There's something to be said for the ease and attractiveness of horizontal broiling, though not much! Experts disagree on horizontal broiling of fish, which isn't unusual. I've always believed that a fish should be broiled on the skin side first (if it's been filleted or cut open from the back, of course) about two-thirds as long as on the flesh side. One of the guides with whom I used to work insists that the flesh side should be broiled first—then the skin side. He says that butter applied to the flesh after turning the fish then melts and runs down through the meat. I never like to argue with a good outdoor cook, and this guide was just that!

At any rate, and by any method of broiling, always season with salt and pepper before broiling and brush generously with butter, bacon fat, or salt pork. Fish that isn't over 1- to 1½-inch thick shouldn't require more than 5 to 7 minutes. If the skin should scorch slightly, don't fret. It'll peel right off.

The simplest method of cooking small fish, of course, is pan frying. In fact, trout up to about 10 or 12 inches are best served up in this way. Modern cook books repeatedly suggest "cooking oils" or "shortening." This is enough to send any good woods cook into a tizzy from which he won't recover for a week! Salt pork and bacon fat are the only agents that are fittin'! As a compromise, you might combine a little butter with bacon grease, but save the cooking oil for lubricating the hinge on a rusty fry pan! I won't get involved in the age-old controversy about whether trout should be fried with or without their heads on. If you leave 'em, you can make a concession to gentility by cutting out the eyes. They stare so! A common mistake when frying fish is to overcook, which dries out the flesh and dissipates flavor. Cook only until the meat becomes flaky. Small trout are inclined to curl in the frying pan, but this can be prevented by breaking the spinal cord at two or three points by running the point of a knife into it. This will cut the flesh slightly, of course, but it does no harm.

Deep-fat frying is less popular in camp since few family campers carry enough grease for this purpose. For tasty deep-frying, however, save the fat from the breakfast bacon in a small can with tight-fitting lid. It keeps well even under mediocre refrigeration. Also, you won't need more than an inch or so in a skillet. A full French fryer isn't necessary. Deep frying serves to seal the exterior of the flesh with a coating which keeps the flesh itself from absorbing grease while it cooks. Usually, some sort of a breaded dip is applied before immersing the fish in the hot fat. This should be smoking hot. Don't immerse too many pieces of fish at once or this will cool the grease and slow cooking so that the flesh will then absorb greasiness. Keep the fat clear of bits of food left over from previous use. Lacking sufficient bacon fat, lard may be used or, best of all, olive oil. This, however, is expensive!

No two woods cooks agree on the ingredient combination for tasty "breading," but I'm sure you'll be happy with the results if you first roll the fish in flour that has been seasoned slightly with salt and pepper. Then dip the fish in beaten eggs. Now, roll it in finely crumbled bread crumbs. Let it dry a while to "fix" the breading, then fry. How long should it cook? That depends upon the size of the pieces and the temperature of the fat. You'll have to experiment. Deep-frying is deceptive, however, and many cooks wait for a deep brown to appear. By the time the fish is removed, it is overdone. Remove it *before* it is browned to a too-dark shade! Use kitchen tongs for lifting from the hot fat. Never stick fish with a fork while it's in hot fat!

Baking is probably at its best with larger fish, 2 pounds

or better, although I've included recipes for smaller ones —which I'm more prone to catching! Baking may be done in a Coleman oven, reflector, or Dutch oven. In the latter two, it's best to place the fish on a small trivet so that it won't scorch on the bottom. The Coleman oven should be kept at moderate temperature. Basting is necessary, not only for flavor but to prevent drying. Much of this can be accomplished by placing slices of bacon or salt pork atop the fish. Its interior, too, should get an application of butter and lemon juice plus salt and pepper. The body cavity may also be filled with a dressing, such as the one described later in this chapter. Most baking is done in some form of liquid: milk, sour cream, or even a tomato sauce. It's a matter of taste. In any event, the liquid should be used for additional basting as baking proceeds.

Boiled fish, as far as I'm concerned, is best suited for baiting mink traps. Actually, no chef worth his paprika boils fish. He simmers it. Some prefer to call it poaching. Otherwise it becomes stringy and tastes like watered-down kapok. Certain "rich" fish, such as lake trout, salmon, and sea-run species, react best to "boiling." Any research on the subject will lead you to an endless array of "court bouillons," laden with various wines and herbs, in which experts advise fish should be poached or simmered. All this is well and good in a well-stocked household kitchen, but in camp you may have to forego these exotic touches. Instead, add ½ teaspoon salt and 1 tablespoon vinegar or lemon juice to each quart of water. If the fish is to be boiled whole, some advise that it be started in cold water. However, I prefer to cut the fish into chunks and drop these directly into boiling water, then slowing the heat to a gentle simmer. A 1-pound fish, cut in two, will cook in 5 to 7 minutes.

Lacking mink traps to bait, boiled fish can be made edible by serving it with an egg sauce. There are dozens of embellished versions of egg sauce in any cookbook, but a simple and basic "starter" can be made by adding enough water to a tablespoon of flour to create a thin paste. Stir this into a cup of water. Heat slowly in a skillet until it starts to thicken. Add two finely chopped hard-boiled eggs and cook slowly until thick. Pour over the fish and serve, seasoned to suit. Some prefer to use milk instead of water and this should be done in a double boiler. Evaporated milk, mixed half-and-half with water, works well.

All of the recipes which follow assume that the fish has been cleaned, head and tail removed, and scales, skin, or fins removed where necessary.

Pan-fried Trout No. 1

Season with salt and pepper. Roll in flour and fry in equal parts of oil and margarine or butter. Bacon fat adds flavor. Cook until skin is crisp. Serve with lemon slice.

Pan-fried Trout No. 2

Contrary to almost every "expert's" assertion, don't wipe trout dry for this recipe. Leave the "slime" on for a flavor treat! Sprinkle with corn meal. Fry in salt pork fat, sizzling hot. Brown on both sides, turning only once. Season and eat—quickly!

Pan-fried Trout No. 3

Wipe fish dry, dip in milk, roll in mixture of flour and corn meal. Fry in cooking oil or butter at moderate heat until meat is flaky, turning often. Garnish with lemon or cucumber and serve immediately.

Deep-fried Crappies

Roll fish in mixture of two parts corn meal and one part flour. Fry in deep fat hot enough so that corn and meal-flour covering browns almost immediately. Drain on a paper towel or brown-paper bag.

Deep-fried Perch

Blend 3 tablespoons of grated process American or Cheddar cheese into 2 beaten eggs. Dip fish in this mixture. Roll in crumbled corn flakes (crumble 'em using a bottle as a rolling pin!). Season with salt and pepper. Deep-fry until browned, probably 5 to 7 minutes in moderately hot fat.

Deep-fried Walleys (Trout or Perch, too)

Roll fish in half-and-half mixture of flour and corn meal,

Deep fry in one part butter and three parts bacon fat that is smoking hot. This is a quick one. Don't fry over 3 minutes!

Baked Fish No. 1

This is a good recipe for small fish such as perch. Brush inside and out with half-and-half mixture of butter and lemon juice, season with salt and pepper. Bake in greased pan in Coleman oven at 400 degrees for 20 to 30 minutes. Suitable for a reflector oven, too, but you'll need a brisk fire and a watchful eye.

Baked Fish No. 2

Also well suited to small fish, up to ½ pound each. Grease tin generously with bacon fat. Lay fish in this and pour 1 tablespoon well-heated bacon fat or drawn butter over each. Sprinkle with finely ground bread crumbs, salt and pepper, and a few drops of lemon juice. Bake 20 minutes at 350 degrees or until browned. Suitable for any camp oven, including cast-iron Dutch oven.

Baked Fish No. 3

This one is for bigger fish, up to about 1 pound. Several can be done at once, of course. Rub with salt inside and out and place in a greased tin. Brush with melted butter and lay one slice of bacon on each fish. Bake 25 to 30 minutes at 375 degrees. For larger fish, prepare and cook as above but add a bread stuffing, inserted into cavity of each fish and made as follows:

1 small chopped onion	1 teaspoon savory
5 tablespoons melted	seasoning
butter	2 tablespoons milk
2 pinches pepper	2 cups bread crumbs

Sauté onions in melted butter. Add seasonings, crumbs, and milk, mixing thoroughly. If chopped celery is available, add about ½ cup. Stuff into body cavities and take one or two turns with string to close and hold in dressing.

Baked Fish No. 4

Dust with salt and pepper inside and out. Place fish in greased tin and add 1 can of tomato soup with about half the usual amount of water added. Bake for 25 to 30 minutes at 400 degrees. If fish is large, use less soup which shouldn't be quite up to the level of the dorsal fin.

Moosehead Racer

A "racer" is a skinny salmon, usually of the land-locked variety. It looks more like a pickerel than the usual deep-bellied Salmo sebago. This recipe applies to a normal salmon, too, but it happens that the first time I saw one cooked in this manner, we'd caught only one fish—a 3-pound racer—and we were hungry. The guide cleaned the fish as usual, cut off head and tail, then cut the fish in two pieces. He lay these in his Dutch oven, after brushing them well with bacon fat—using his fingers! Then he added an inch of diluted evaporated milk and a dash of vinegar. "Give it a nice sour cream taste," he explained. He salted the fish and sprinkled on enough pepper to make a moose sneeze. Up to this point, it was all very unappetizing. This was before I'd become a guide myself. He placed the Dutch oven in the rough stone fireplace after heaping hot coals onto the cover. A half hour later I was hungry enough to try the salmon. I wasn't sorry. We cleaned it up, along with a batch of pan-baked corn bread!

Baked Fish 'n' Chips

2 cups crumbled potato chips	1 can mushroom soup
1 teaspoon butter or margarine	1 cup milk
	1 can salmon (red)

Mix the soup, milk, and salmon and bring to a simmer in a skillet or saucepan. Add butter, stirring in until well blended. Pour into a greased tin, sprinkle on potato chips, and bake at 350 degrees for 25 minutes. Cooked fresh fish may be substituted for the salmon. That empty salmon can won't add much status to a fisherman's campsite!

Pocahontas Pickerel

This is a novelty recipe for those looking for fun as well as good eating. Don't scale or skin the pickerel—one preferably about 2 pounds. Find a long, narrow stone that will fit into the fish's body cavity. Heat the stone piping hot over your campfire. With kitchen tongs, insert it into the fish, after having brushed the interior with butter and salt. Wrap the fish in several loose layers of heavy-duty foil and bury it in the coals and ashes of your campfire. It'll take about a half hour, but it won't hurt the fish to stay a little longer if it's a large one. When you open the package, the skin will peel off, the hot rock will slip out, and the flaky whitened meat will part from the bony critter easily. This is for campers who like to gamble, since I must confess to an occasional failure because the stone was not hot enough!

Done-by-Dawn Trout

It doesn't *have* to be trout. Any fish up to about a pound will do. Season with salt and pepper inside and out and seal each fish individually in several layers of aluminum foil. Place in a hole *beneath* your campsite fireplace so that it's covered by 1 to 1½ inches of earth. Build your evening campfire, enjoy coffee, watch the moon, then go to bed. By breakfast time, the fish will be done!

Finny Hash

2 tablespoons chopped onion	1 teaspoon salt
3 cups cooked fish	⅛ teaspoon pepper
3 cups boiled potatoes	⅓ cup bacon fat

Fish should be free of bones; potatoes diced. Mix these with onion and seasonings. Form into round patties ¾-inch thick and fry. Brown on both sides. Serves four.

POST-MORTEMS

One of the advantages of cooking your fish, apart from a lot of good eating, is that you destroy what might be highly controversial evidence against you in the recounting of the catch. Fish have a way of growing with years, and while "Allah does not deduct from the allotted span of man those hours spent in fishing," he does frown upon outlandish growth long after a fish has been eaten. A fisherman is entitled to the natural growth of a fish he has caught—and no more!

Chapter XIX

Desserts
and Gooey
Snacks

DESSERTS in camp take on many forms—fruit, candy, pastries, berries, pudding. In fact, almost any food that satisfies a craving for sweets can qualify, and thanks to modern food processing, the variety for family campers is practically unlimited. With a supermarket nearly always within driving distance, it's easy to restock often on candy and "store-bought" pastries. However, when the cook is imaginative and ingenious, his family is in for real treats. When it comes to concocting gooey goodies, however, I bow to the Girl Scouts! Give 'em a few dried crackers, a teaspoon of sugar, and hot water and they'll somehow come up with a calorie-laden Caramel Heart's Desire on a Stick that reduces me to a drooling idiot! In fact, after dining with Girl Scouts, I'm likely to waddle away like a pregnant porcupine! The recipes that follow are along these imaginative, bold, and fearless lines.

Tenderfoot Cake

2 cups flour	½ teaspoon salt
2 eggs	½ cup butter or margarine
1 cup sugar	¾ cup milk
2½ teaspoons baking powder	1 teaspoon vanilla

Sift baking powder, flour, and salt together. Beat eggs and add to melted butter and sugar. Blend flour and egg mixture, adding milk and vanilla. Beat gently but thoroughly. Bake in greased 8" x 8" tin for 35-40 minutes at 350 degrees, or before brisk fire in reflector oven.

Cake Pan Chocolate Cake

Sift into an 8-inch square pan:

1½ cups sifted all-purpose flour	3 tablespoons cocoa
1 cup sugar	1 teaspoon baking soda
	½ teaspoon salt

Make three holes in the mixture. Into the first, pour 6 tablespoons melted shortening or salad oil. Into the second, 1 tablespoon vinegar. Into the third, 1 teaspoon vanilla. Pour 1 cup cold water over all and stir with a fork until well blended. Bake at 350 degrees for 35-40 minutes in Coleman oven. This cake keeps well but doesn't last long. It is moist and is best frosted in the pan.

Skillet Nut Coffeecake

This can be baked in a skillet if you lack an oven. Prepare coffeecake mix as directed on package. Form aluminum foil pan, pour the mixture into it and sprinkle with ⅓ cup chopped walnuts. Place foil pan on trivet or inverted pie plate in heated skillet and cover. Bake on fireplace grill over low fire 35 minutes.

Blueberry Pie

If there's anything tastier in camp than a blueberry pie whose juices run down your chin, I haven't tried it! Use a pie crust mix if you like. Bake the lower crust first, empty. Then fill it with freshly picked blueberries. Add about ¾ cup of sugar and a few dabs of butter, dash in a bit of cinnamon, then sprinkle well with flour. Cover with the top crust, wet and seal the edges, cut slits in it and bake in Coleman oven at 425 degrees for about 30 minutes or until top crust is browned.

Lacking a pie crust mix, you can make pie crust as it's made in lumbercamps, from a few ingredients carried in most camp kitchen boxes. Mix ½ teaspoon baking powder with ½ teaspoon salt and 1 cup of flour. Blend in ⅓ cup of lard. Add cold water until you have proper consistency for rolling.

Apple Pie

1 can apples or	2 tablespoons butter
½ dozen fresh apples	½ teaspoon cinnamon
Pie crust mix	½ cup sugar

Mix pie crust according to directions or use the lumberman's recipe above. Even gramma's recipe will do! Form lower crust into pie plate, lay in apples, spread sugar over these, sprinkle with cinnamon and dab here and there with butter. Add top crust, wetting and sealing edges. Cut slits in top. Bake at 425 degrees for 40 minutes. A teaspoon of cornstarch added before "closing" the pie is supposed to keep the juices from overflowing. It usually works.

Blueberry Squares

3 cups flour	2 teaspoons baking powder
2 sticks butter or	1 teaspoon vanilla
margarine	2 eggs
1½ cups sugar	

Combine ingredients and with pastry blender or two knives, cut until mixture is crumbly. Press half of it into ungreased 9- by 13-inch pan. Spread one can blueberry pie filling (or other fruit or berry filling) over crumbs. Cover with remaining crumb mixture. Bake at 375 degrees 30 to 35 minutes. Cool and cut into squares.

Pecan Confections

2 egg whites	¼ teaspoon salt
2 cups brown sugar	2 cups chopped pecans
2 tablespoons flour	

Beat egg whites to stiff froth. Add sugar gradually. Sift flour and salt over egg whites and sugar. Make "sort of a meringue." Fold in. Stir in pecans. Drop by the teaspoonful on greased cooky sheet or aluminum foil at least two inches apart. Bake at 300 degrees 15 to 20 minutes. Makes about 5 dozen.

Orange Upside-down Biscuits

Make a sauce of 1 cup of orange juice, ½ cup sugar and 2 tablespoons butter. Put in skillet and allow to boil down a little, being careful not to burn. Prepare 2 cups biscuit mix according to directions. Pat flat, spread dough with butter, sugar, and cinnamon. Roll and cut into slices one inch thick. Place in sauce and bake until golden brown. Serve upside-down with butter. Serves four.

Cherry Cobbler

2 cups pitted cherries	2 cups flour
1½ cups sugar	3 tablespoons baking powder
1 cup milk	4 tablespoons butter
½ cup hot water	1 teaspoon salt

Combine baking powder, salt, milk, flour, and ¾ cup sugar. Pour into greased tin, add sugar and hot water to cherries and pour over batter. Bake at 350 degrees for 40 minutes.

Short-cut Fruit Pudding

Cover bottom of greased tin with heavily buttered slices of bread. Old or stale bread may be used. Over these, pour one can of sliced peaches, pears or other fruit, including syrup. Sprinkle with brown sugar. Bake 25 minutes at 350 to 375 degrees. Serve with syrup or milk.

Blueberry Dumplings

Simmer blueberries in water and sugar until they start to soften. Have water level well below that of berries and sweeten to taste. Mix dough from prepared biscuit mix. Lay gobs on top of stewing blueberries and cover kettle partially. Cook until "dumplings" are done. One quart blueberries to ½ dozen small dumplings is a good proportion.

Lemon Custard

Mix in skillet:	1 tablespoon flour
¾ cup sugar	3 tablespoons lemon juice

Bring to a boil, then pour over 3 beaten eggs in bowl.

Return to skillet and cook a few minutes longer, stirring until thickened. Serves four, warm or cold.

Skillet Shortcake

Use favorite recipe to make 4 large pancakes. Add 1 egg to mix to make them "fluffy." Stack these with canned applesauce and a liberal sprinkling of confectioner's sugar between layers. Cut in sections and serve hot.

Frying Pan Cookies

1 cup brown sugar	1 cup chopped dates
2 eggs, beaten	

Mix together and cook in frying pan 10 minutes, stirring constantly. Remove from heat and add 2 cups Rice Krispies. Drop by spoonfuls onto waxed paper or aluminum foil and roll in shredded coconut. Do not bake. Makes one dozen.

Peanut Crunchies

3 cups crisp, sugar-coated corn cereal	½ pound (32) marshmallov
2 squares unsweetened chocolate	½ cup chunk-style peanut]
	⅓ cup butter

Combine butter, peanut butter, marshmallows, and chocolate in pan. Cook over low heat and stir until ingredients are melted and well blended. Remove from fire, add cereal, mixing well. Pat into 8-inch square pan and allow to stand until cool. Cut into bars.

Chocolate Oatmeal Cookies

2 cups sugar	½ cup milk
½ cup cocoa	¼ pound margarine
Pinch of salt	

Combine ingredients and boil 3½ minutes. Remove from heat, add 4 cups quick-cooking oats *or* 3 cups oats and 1 cup shredded coconut. Stir until oats are completely covered. Drop on waxed paper. Allow a few minutes to cool and harden. Makes 1½-2 dozen.

Oatmeal Fudgies

Put in 2 quart saucepan:
½ cup milk
2 cups sugar
½ cup cocoa
¼ pound margarine

Mix over heat and bring to a full boil for 1 minute. Remove from heat and add:
1 teaspoon vanilla
½ cup peanut butter

Mix well, then add:
2½ cups quick-cooking. oatmeal
½ cup raisins

Mix well and drop by the teaspoonful on waxed paper. Makes about 6 dozen small cookies.

Marshmallow Cornflake Delights

½ pound (32) marshmallows
¼ pound butter
3 cups cornflakes

Melt marshmallows over low heat, stirring constantly. Remove from heat, add cornflakes, and mix well. Moisten hands in cold water and form mixture into small balls. Place on waxed paper and allow to stand until firm. Makes about 2 dozen.

Bread Pudding with Caramel Sauce

Generously butter and then cube 4 or 5 slices of white bread. Place in top of double boiler. Add 1 cup brown sugar. Over this, pour 3 well-beaten eggs, 2 cups of milk, and 1 teaspoon vanilla. Cover and cook over water until done. Test by inserting knife. If the knife comes out clean, pudding is done.

Mock Angel Cake

Dip day-old bread into sweet condensed milk, then into shredded coconut and toast on fireplace grill over coals until coconut is golden brown.

Two-minute Fudge

2 cups sugar	2 tablespoons cornstarch
½ cup milk	2 tablespoons cocoa
Butter, size of a walnut	1 teaspoon vanilla

Cook without stirring until mixture comes to a hard boil. Boil for 2 minutes. Remove from heat and add vanilla. Beat until gloss disappears and pour into buttered pan. For variety, add 2 heaping tablespoons marshmallow fluff *or* 1 cup of chopped nuts. Add marshmallows while beating.

Campfire Popcorn

There's a high average of failures with the traditional wire basket corn popper. To make the world's fluffiest and tastiest popcorn, put 3 heaping tablespoons of shortening into the largest of your aluminum cook-kit kettles. Heat this until it smokes. Cover the bottom with popping corn. Put on the cover and shake by the handle over a hot fire or a high flame on the camp stove. Keep shaking until the corn pops. Have patience—keep shaking! You may need an asbestos glove or pot holder. When popped, it'll fill the kettle. Slather on at least ¼ pound of butter or margarine and salt to suit. I prefer yellow corn but the small white is tasty, too. At the risk of my ego showing, I consider myself the master of the corn popper. *This* is the best method!

There's a trick to storing popcorn. If left in the sealed container it will not pop as well as if it's opened a day or so beforehand and allowed to absorb atmospheric moisture. Store it in a glass jar whose lid has been punctured by two or three small holes. Try this. It works, so help me!

Chapter XX

Grub
Lists
and
Menus

READING some of the menus and grub lists suggested to
family campers, you'd think that the average American
camping family spends its summers in the hinterlands of
Tibet. Food lists repeatedly suggest dried applesauce,
powdered eggs, compressed meats, concentrated fruit
juice, citrus crystals, malted milk tablets, and dehydrated
diced potatoes. Doesn't it ever occur to the compilers of
these lists that a camper might enjoy a simple hot dog—
complete with mustard and relish—or a hamburger, or
possibly sausage and pancakes? Family camping foods
need not *all* be dried, compressed, dehydrated, concentrated, or even canned!

One family camping manual goes so far as to supply a
menu-planning chart, made up of orderly little squares
into which the trip planner is supposed to indicate the
per-day number of servings of foods that run the gamut
from powdered fruit juice to malted milk tablets. There's
one little square for each day of the proposed trip and
their totals are then tabulated in a subcolumn from which
cans, 1-pound boxes, 5-pound bags, and 7-ounce tubes!
are figured the number of servings available in 12-ounce
Frankly, the designer lost me several turns back despite
the fact that he clearly pointed out that there are 12 eggs
in a dozen. Holy old catamount! The Allies invaded
France with less fuss than this!

Practically every camping manual advises that campers

plot a day-by-day menu in advance, and this is well and good for those of staunch character who can stick to such menus. I've planned many of these for wilderness trips, but, somehow, they all go awry. For example, how can I know, weeks in advance, that I'll want bacon and eggs on the morning of the second Tuesday? I've been known to ignore my chart and gobble up a can of beans that was meant for Thursday's supper. This has always set off a chain reaction that eventually found me observing my third Sabbath of the trip by dining on parsnip stew and a slice of zwieback found in the side pocket of my rucksack!

For extended trips into the wilderness, such planning is obviously necessary, but so far as family camping is concerned, it can be dispensed with to advantage. Actually, a family camper during the course of any one day's travel, will drive past no fewer than a dozen supermarkets, to say nothing of farmers' fruit and vegetable stands. With such convenience for food shopping, he can play it by ear all the way, giving in to almost any culinary impulse or whim.

This doesn't mean, however, that a camper can breeze through a supermarket and pick up at random whatever catches his eye or sets his salivary glands to exuding. Some planning is necessary; otherwise he's liable to be driving into town for a forgotten 2-ounce package of onion flakes!

Practical camp meal planning centers about the kitchen box which most campers tote along in one form or another. A sound approach is to keep on hand, in this box, many of the staples—seasonings, condiments, and basic ingredients—for which a housewife reaches automatically while getting meals at home. Most of these are nonperishable or nearly so. They can be transferred from the household kitchen shelf to the chuck box, or as many campers do, an entire assortment can be purchased specifically for stocking the camp box. In this case, the "large economy" size isn't necessarily the best choice. Smaller, more compact, units help reduce bulk and weight.

The list in the Appendix isn't intended for use in its entirety. Few families will find use for *all* of the suggestions and probably no chuck box could hold them all. It is a reminder—a check list for stocking *your* chuck box with items *you* will need. I long ago gave up making specific recommendations for food lists. There's always someone who wants to make a change. (No one has ever suggested a perfect list to me, either.)

As a general rule, any staple which is used regularly or frequently in the preparation of simpler meals at home will probably be needed sometime during a two-week car camping trip. For example, some are practically indispensable—baking powder, catsup, coffee, tea, mayonnaise, pancake mix, peanut butter, salt, sugar. On the other hand, you may like to flavor peas with mint for home meals, but, if this is mint's only use in camp, it can probably be dispensed with. Some chefs will want to tote along a full range of herbs and spices, while others will get along with salt and pepper—though heaven help their victims!

For well-rounded and satisfying meals in camp, we'll need more than staples. My own formula for stocking the camp commissary is contrary to the usual procedure which calls for planning a day-by-day menu and then calculating a food list accordingly. I prefer to stock what I call the "stand-bys," some of which are meals in themselves and some merely ingredients, to be used according to the whims and desires of the moment. For a "campground-hopping" trip, with one-night stops, my own family rarely carries more than a three-day supply of these "stand-bys," nearly all of which are nonperishables. The perishable main courses such as fresh meats, along with milk and garden vegetables, we pick up as they are needed.

This may seem a "hind to" approach, but it makes sense. Even if on rare occasions we are unable to obtain fresh meats, milk, and vegetables each day, we can still produce a passable meal from the chuck box! Food spoilage is eliminated, our perishables are *always* fresh, and we have more room in the car. It's far from a hand-to-mouth existence. In fact, it's a rather posh, high-on-the-hog type of camping!

All our camping isn't necessarily confined to campground hopping. Some years we prefer to stay in one spot, in which case we revert to formula. Here the logistics are

156

similar to those of wilderness camping in remote areas. It becomes necessary to plan approximate daily menus, but we add at least three full extra meals per week so that we can avoid being bound to a pre-planned menu. The extra meals allow us to do a certain amount of juggling, and this adds spice to meals. It wasn't always so, however. I recall a two-week canoe trip which Eleanor and I ended with one can of tuna fish on the morning of our last day out. We paddled all day on it and I've never since wanted tuna fish for breakfast!

The list of stand-bys in the Appendix can be used for either type of trip—campground hopping or for a long stay in a remote area. Bear in mind that this list is *not* suitable for use in planning a wilderness trip. For this purpose, I would rely on freeze-dried foods.

The easy availability of fresh foods, principally meats, vegetables, and milk, means that today campers can enjoy practically as tasty and nourishing meals in camp as they do at home. Balanced diets have replaced the 3 B's; children get fresh milk, adults their daily allotment of proteins and greens. Some may snort at this as being overly posh, but given a choice between freeze-dried grub and garden-fresh peas, green beans, corn-on-the-cob, plus a 2-inch broiled steak, I'll leave the dehydrated stuff on the shelf!

Despite its convenience, however, it's not always easy to plan meals around fresh foods. The cut of meat in the supermarket may not appeal to the shopper; the peas may be "gone by" or the sweet corn not quite "filled out," and some flexibility must be allowed, just as it is in the planning of household meals.

Meats which are popular and feasible in camp are those prepared with a minimum of effort. Heavy or large cuts, such as roasts or whole fowl and chickens, will find favor only among dedicated camp chefs who make a hobby of cooking. The most practical fresh meats are beefsteak ground beef or hamburger, ham, pork steak, chops, and sausage (links and country-style), lamb chops, frankfurters, cold cuts for sandwiches, and chicken (cut in ready-to-use pieces). Except for the beefsteak, all of these should be cooked as soon after purchase as possible. I don't mean this in terms of minutes of course, but with the usual camp refrigeration, none will keep well more than 48 hours.

Vegetables which should be purchased no more than a few hours before eating include sweet corn, fresh lettuce, cucumbers, celery, green and waxed beans, radishes, asparagus, and peas. Sea foods also are best "right off the boat," including shrimp, clams, lobster, oysters, and, of course, fish. Even though berries may keep well, they will never again be as palate-tickling as during the first few hours following their harvest.

All fresh foods are to supplement the "stand-bys"; they should be purchased when as fresh as possible and eaten soon thereafter. Storing freshly picked peas, for example, is like showing up at the stadium on Monday morning with a pair of tickets on the 50-yard line.

It used to be good planning to purchase as much camping food as possible at a neighborhood store. Prices were generally lower, you were surer of quality, and you could buy brands you knew. To some degree, this is still true. However, supermarkets are now everywhere, and their volume of business, plus modern packaging and marketing methods, have pretty much standardized prices. Brands, too, are usually nationally distributed. Small, isolated, country stores generally charge higher prices, as do stores maintained on campgrounds. But their locations close by may be much more convenient than a distant supermarket. Buying food "on the road," all in all, is far more convenient, even if it does cost you a few cents more per day to eat!

The old belief that farm prices are much lower than city prices for fresh vegetables and fruits no longer is valid. Farmers get daily market quotations, too! Though prices may not be notably lower in the country, freshness and quality are more of a certainty. Roadside stands don't always sell "garden-fresh" foods, however. Many of these, particularly the big, "flashy-front" type, are often nothing more than retail outlets with much of the produce purchased from wholesalers and possibly even hauled in from another state! If you want really fresh fruits and vegetables, look for the smaller roadside stand, usually a temporary structure open only following local harvests. Near my permanent tent site, there's a farmer who has a sign by the roadside only during the sweet corn season. He takes your order, then picks it while you wait! His prices are at market level, but what supermarket can claim *that* kind of freshness for its foods?

Canned goods and dried foods can be stocked economically during the winter by taking advantage of supermarket specials during "six-for-a-dollar" offers on various canned foods, and by buying one or two extra items for use the following summer. Set these aside and your camp pantry will be well stocked with most of the "stand-bys" when next year's vacation time rolls around. You'll be "toting heavy," it's true, but you will probably have saved enough for an extra 400 or 500 miles of vacation travel. Also, you will have eliminated a burdensome lump-sum outlay for food at vacation time. The disadvantage of this, however, is that you'll have a heavily loaded car going down the road to vacationland!

One of the reasons I persistently refuse to suggest specific menus is that I feel means should be planned around activities and according to the weather, as well, of course, as the eating inclinations of the moment. The following meals are *suggestions* which permit this flexibility.

BREAKFASTS

Breakfast menus are traditionally centered around fruits and juices, cereals, eggs, bacon, ham, sausage, flapjacks, muffins, toast, coffee or cocoa. There's more than tradition involved, however. These foods taste good in the morning and they supply energy for the day's living.

If it's going to be a warm, lazy day in which our greatest exertion will consist of watching the kids make mudpies on the beach, breakfast will be light, possibly including fruit juice or canned grapefruit sections, corn flakes in milk, coffee or cocoa.

If the morning is cold or my family is planning to climb up Lookout Mountain after breakfast, we'll naturally eat heartily, probably including the following:

Orange juice, canned or crystals
Flapjacks with syrup and butter or margarine
Bacon or sausage
Coffee or cocoa

Or, we may decide that the climb to the fire tower is a
really tough one. Then, we'll probably have:

Fruit juice, canned or crystals
Country-style sausage (it may even be freeze-dried!)
Fried potatoes
Scrambled eggs
Muffins with butter, jam or jelly
Coffee or cocoa

LUNCHES

I suppose my feelings concerning lunch are a carry-over
from my days as a woods guide. Woodsmen eat lightly at
noon, quite often nothing more than a sandwich or two
and possibly a little tea steeped over a quick fire. There's
sound reasoning behind this. Lengthier meal preparations
eat into travel time, and you can't tote a heavy pack or
pole a canoe through rapids all afternoon if you're gorged
on a heavy meal. True, we were often "gaunt in the mid-
dle" by late afternoon, but a full-fledged supper took care
of that. Lying around a campfire in the evening wasn't a
difficult chore even on a slightly overfilled stomach, and
while this probably wasn't sound dietary behavior, it *was*
fun!

Family camping lunches might wisely parallel those of
the woodsman, especially since light meals are quickly
prepared, thus freeing the camp cook for his or her share
of the afternoon's fun. Lunch might include sandwiches,
fruit, and a beverage, with hot soup for cold days.

When older children, especially teenagers, are in the
group, you may be required to serve up a more substantial
meal. Even this can be kept simple, easily and quickly
prepared with, perhaps, Sloppy Joes (Chapter XXIII),
mixed vegetable salad with dressing, and soft drinks,
coffee or tea.

SUPPER

Supper in camp is usually between five and six P.M. Children are ravenous by that time and there still remains plenty of daylight after the meal for doing dishes. This is the meal which should be governed by the campers' fancies and one where the cook can express himself through the medium of his skill with pot, ladle, and a dash of paprika, and for which he reaches into his bag of tricks. If he's lacking an idea momentarily, I'll go only so far as to suggest that he pore through some of the recipes in Chapter XXIII.

FROZEN FOODS

I haven't touched upon these for the simple reason that they are so commonplace in household kitchens that I hesitate to advise a housewife on the subject! The variety is great and the flavor of juices, meats, and vegetables, well-known. They are feasible in camping only insofar as they are handily available for immediate use. If the campground store carries them, by all means enjoy them. They can even be transported for a few hours without thawing too much, by insulating them with heavy wrappings of paper or by storing them in dry ice in the camp refrigerator. Generally, however, they do not keep well once thawed and should be used as soon as possible. No doubt, as I write this, some brilliant young engineer is at work in his garret designing a portable camp food freezer. When he succeeds, and I'm sure he will, frozen foods will come into their own for camping purposes.

Chapter XXI

Tableware

While camping alone and living out of my knapsack, I've usually eaten my meals directly from my skillet or cook pot. This saves washing one plate. Expeditious as this may be, it's hardly a gracious form of dining even in camp. Fortunately, family camping has brought some of the little amenities to the campsite.

Among these is the use of a tablecloth. A generation ago, this would have brought guffaws from "dyed-in-the-wool" campers, but today it's hardly worth a second glance except to observe that a tablecloth not only lends neatness to a picnic table, but it also makes outdoor meals more attractive and appetizing. Early family campers used oilcloth, and many still do, since it is easy to clean. However, in cool weather it will crack if folded. Rolling it makes too cumbersome a package. More widely in use nowadays is plastic, easily cleaned and so inexpensive that it can be discarded after each trip or at the end of the season. Rolling it, folding it, or stuffing it into a kettle doesn't hurt it, and it's colorful. Old bed sheets and used shower curtains are often proposed, too, but these suggestions somehow lack conviction—and acceptance!

The wind has an annoying habit of blowing a tablecloth up over the table, usually just as the cook sets a platter of something gooey within reach of the flapping corners. We used to sew a pocket into each corner of the tablecloth and a small stone inserted into each of these kept the table's cover in place. Later, we learned about trouser clips used by bicycle riders. More recently an alert plastics manufacturer developed a plastic counterpart of the bicycle clip which holds tablecloths in place.

A tablecloth isn't a necessity, of course. Dispensing with it, you can use roll paper towels or aluminum foil for place mats, or paper napkins.

Picnic tables at campsites aren't always large enough if there are several children in the family. Too, some sites are without tables. For such exigencies, take along a folding aluminum table, preferably a 6-footer. Folding chairs, too, can be carried, but several of them may prove too bulky to pack into a car. (Actually, I prefer to straddle a log or squat on a stump.)

Camp meals are more often than not served via a "chow line," directly from the cook pot into the dining plate, but if some sort of a serving platter is used, provision must be made for keeping the meal hot until it is served. A warming oven is not far-fetched, since these are lightweight, compact, and inexpensive. Most camping-equipment catalogs list them. Lacking such an oven, "seconds" can be kept warm by overlaying them with a hood of aluminum foil and leaving them on the fireplace or camp stove. A common kitchen roaster makes an ideal warming oven. While it may be bulky to pack, the space it occupies need not be wasted. Pack smaller items in the roaster. For small quantities of food, one plate inverted over another will serve.

The variety of dining plates is wide. Most newcomers to camping assume that the aluminum plates included in cook kits or ordinary tin plates will nicely serve the purpose, only to learn that these carry heat away from food so rapidly that it becomes a race to eat a hamburger patty before it becomes cemented to the plate by hardening grease. Disposable aluminum plates are little improvement and their cost will mount rapidly in a family of six during a two-week vacation! Enamelware will hold heat well when preheated and is as easy to wash as china, but the grade currently on the market is susceptible to chipping.

Disposable paper plates will absorb liquids quickly and are inclined to disintegrate. The plastic-coated paper plates are a definite improvement in this respect, but a steak knife cuts through them easily. Plastic seems to hold the answer to the problem but beware of lightweight picnic-grade plates. These will warp out of shape or even melt if exposed to a hot stew! Probably one of the finest of the synthetic plates is Melmac, a heavy-duty, colorful tableware with a hard, glazed surface comparable to that of sturdy china.

When I worked in lumbercamps, we were given one 9-inch tin pie plate from which to eat our meals. It even served as a soup bowl. Family campers needn't suffer such Spartanism, however. The number of plastic soup and cereal bowls on the market is nearly countless. All supply houses have them.

Campers long ago learned that aluminum cups burned their lips, even after the liquid had cooled to acceptable levels, and these are now omitted from cook kits, having been replaced by plastic. For years, our family has been drinking coffee from ceramic mugs, our present set of 6 now in its seventh year of use without a replacement. They're not as easily broken as some would have you think, although they are somewhat heavy. Enamelware cups are also available although I've searched in vain during recent years for a set with open handles which would allow the cups to nest. Paper cups are satisfactory, but their cost mounts during an extended camping trip.

Probably the cleverest kit on the market is the Taffell camping set, made of polystyrene. It consists of a 2-gallon carrying case which can be used for toting water; a 6½-pint lid which is suggested as a wash basin, but which is better suited as a serving dish; four plates deep enough to double as soup bowls and recessed in one corner to hold a triangular tumbler. Also included in the set are three kitchen canisters ranging from ½ to 1½ pints and ideal for storing leftovers. While the set is designed for four persons, extra tumblers and plates may be purchased separately.

Given a choice of dinnerware and drinking cups, I would choose enamelware, the Taffell or Melmac materials, tin, then—and only in desperation—aluminum.

"Chow sets," a teaspoon, knife, and fork nesting one into the other and fitting into an individual simulated-leather or plastic case, are popular. However, I much prefer a galley kit. This consists of a compartmented cloth, usually light drill, which holds stainless-steel table silver, along with a spatula, ladle, pancake turner, basting spoon, and kitchen tongs, each in its own compartment. The cloth is rolled and tied shut, thus enclosing the implements for transportation. Like all fine equipment, the outfit is expensive, selling for about 20 dollars. However, there's no reason why a clever seamstress can't make a similar cloth container which she can then fill with inexpensive "dime-store" tableware and utensils. In buying inexpensive knives, forks, and spoons, however, don't buy those with plastic handles. The stuff can't stand rinsing in boiling water.

Camp-type aluminum salt and pepper shakers should be carried since these can be closed to avoid spilling. Some are single units which dispense both salt and pepper. Lacking these, the regular miniature shaker-containers sold in markets will serve as well.

Polystyrene or polyethylene canisters with snug-fitting lids are ideal for refrigerating or storing leftovers. One firm puts out an "insulated" type, much like a thermos bottle. Too, there are plastic jars with screw-on caps, in various sizes. There's even a polystyrene (or is it polyethylene?) cooky jar, a condiment dispenser for catsup, mustard, et cetera, a juice set which includes a decanter and drinking glasses—all lightweight, unbreakable, inexpensive, and with snug-fitting lids, though I doubt that the covers are snug enough to defy some 10-year-old ice chest raider!

A hot mat should also be provided. Placing a hot dish or pot on a plastic tablecloth will ruin it and may even blister the paint on the picnic table. We use an aluminum-covered asbestos mat which doubles as an insulator under baking tins in our Coleman oven to prevent scorching certain foods. If you prefer, there are all sorts of wire grids on short legs which may be used in place of asbestos.

Don't overlook a dishpan. All women are acquainted with the variety that's available in colorful plastic or hard rubber, ideal for camping. Some have a rinsing compartment, although I've heard several women complain that this is too small to be worthwhile. Several families I know carry two single-compartment dishpans, one nesting into the other. They wash in one, rinse in the other. Carry soap powders, dish mop or cloth, scouring pads, in the dishpan when traveling. Don't forget dish towels.

Chapter XXII

Tricks
of the
Camp Cook

A CAMP COOK's "tricks" make the rounds like a good story, the point of origin soon becoming lost in the telling and retelling. Trying to credit originators for these helpful hints would require the publishing of another book, devoted solely to the culinary wisdom of housewives, guides, lumbercamp cooks, campers, cowboys, professional chefs, Indians, forest rangers, miners, game wardens, and dozens of others. Nevertheless, I should point out that few, if any, of the following tips were originated by me. Someone, somewhere, passed them on to me, and I can only say to them, "I've passed 'em along!"

Housewives, of course, have hundreds of little "gimmicks" that are useful about a home kitchen, and I've included here only those which are also applicable to camp cooking:

To impart a barbecue flavor to broiled meats, sprinkle them lightly with instant coffee.

Mix powdered whole milk in a screw-top jar or friction-top can.

If your pie crust tastes "lardy," add a pinch of ginger next time.

Add a little cornstarch to sugar to prevent juices from running out of fruit pies.

To sour milk quickly, add a few drops of vinegar or lemon juice.

Add a pinch or two of salt to water when boiling a

cracked egg to prevent white from running out, or wrap the egg tightly in aluminum foil.

A pinch of flour sprinkled on fat while frying will stop the spattering.

During the winter, save those TV dinner trays for camp dishes. Saves washing at the campsite and you can discard them after using them.

A 2½-gallon plastic-bag-in-a-carton milk container makes an excellent water dispenser in camp.

If you fear your gasoline stove's "POOF" when you ignite it, hold a lighted wooden match in a pair of kitchen tongs.

Use a round soft-drink bottle for a rolling pin and your overturned canoe or the hood of your car for a pastry board.

A small soft-drink bottle can be used for a potato masher. Lacking a bottle, use a small billet of wood.

Putting a small dab of butter in oatmeal while it's cooking will make the pot much easier to clean.

Removing single strips of sliced bacon from a package is difficult. Roll the package tightly. The slices will come off easily.

On a cold day, butter may be too hard to spread easily. Invert a heated bowl or pan over the butter dish for a few minutes. This will soften the butter, but not melt it.

Does the picnic table smell fishy after cleaning a mess of trout or bass? Sprinkle ordinary table salt to remove the odor. Wash it clean before night, however, as porcupines love salt and will chew the table!

For French fries, use old potatoes. New spuds don't brown well.

Save the liquid when you've eaten the contents of a jar of sweet pickles. It adds a delicious flavor to green beans, potato salad, fish, and other foods.

You can prevent thick stews, cereals, and other such foods from sticking to the kettle by adding a dozen small pebbles which have been rinsed. Be careful when serving, pebbles are tough on teeth!

Biscuits, breads, and corncakes which are dried out can be freshened by placing in a brown paper bag after sprinkling lightly with water. Place the bag in your heated Coleman a few minutes.

Stale doughnuts regain their fresh-out-of-the-fat flavor by being similarly heated in an oven.

To remove fishy odor from your hands, rub a little vinegar on them, then rinse in cold water. The same can be done for frying pans.

Flapjacks won't be inclined to stick to the griddle or skillet if you add a tablespoon of melted fat to each 1½ cups of batter.

To keep slab bacon from moulding, wrap in cheesecloth that has been wet with vinegar.

You can brighten the interior of a darkened aluminum kettle any one of several ways. Heat a weak solution of water and vinegar or cream of tartar in it, or cook grape jelly—or boil apple parings—or prunes, especially when lemon juice has been added. The kettle will turn shiny and bright.

Sprinkle a few drops of water on sliced bacon to keep it from shriveling in the frying pan.

Even though it's done in the movies and on TV, don't wash pots and pans with cold water and sand. There's no substitute for hot water and soap.

A collapsible wire salad basket helps in washing vegetables, fruits, and salad greens. It can double as a hot mat when collapsed.

To prevent a musty smell in a camp ice chest as a result of long disuse, keep a cake of unwrapped Ivory soap in it, or use an old Navy trick. Sprinkle the bottom of the chest with regular-grind coffee. Don't use instant coffee. It'll absorb moisture and make a gooey mess.

If strongly flavored foods have been cooked in fat or oil, cool the fat partially, add a few pieces of raw potato and reheat. The potato will absorb the strong flavor. Discard this and strain the fat through a cloth.

To tenderize tough cuts of beef, as for a stew, add a little vinegar to the water in which the meat is being boiled.

Cheese cut in strips or narrow slices will keep well in a glass jar kept covered.

French toast is tenderer if water instead of milk is mixed with eggs.

Olives won't spoil in an opened bottle if a teaspoon of olive oil is added.

A little vinegar will remove onion odor from a skillet.

Drop a small pad of butter in with spaghetti to prevent boiling over.

Scrambled eggs go farther if bread crumbs are added.

Dill pickles will keep longer without mold if the jar is shaken once a day.

A little lemon juice added to the boiling water will make rice whiter and keep the grains separated.

Eggs, dipped in boiling water for ten seconds, will last for weeks in a camp ice chest.

Cake and bread will stay fresher for longer if half an apple is placed in the bread box. Change the apple occasionally.

Bouillon cubes can be substituted for meat stock in making camp soups.

Rub fat trimmings or a strip of bacon over a basket broiler to keep meats from sticking to the grill.

Hamburgers should be handled gently. They're tenderer if patted into shape, rather than pressed.

For an accurate measure, brown sugar must be packed firmly into a measuring cup.

If vegetables or cereal scorch, plunge the pan and all into cold water for a few minutes. Much of the burned taste will be dissipated.

Never beat a pancake batter. Stir it and don't worry about the lumps. They'll disappear.

Save canned vegetable liquids and boil until reduced about half. Add ½ cup of milk and some flour for a rich sauce.

Cut biscuits or cookies with the cover of a baking powder can.

Doesn't sound logical, but you can carry fresh eggs by breaking them into one of those narrow olive jars so that they are "stacked." They'll pour out one at a time, too.

In broiling, don't cook meats or other foods directly on discarded refrigerator or stove shelves. Some of these are cadmium-plated and may cause violent illness through poisoning.

Butter will keep for a long time when packed in sterilized jars with tight-fitting screw-top lids.

Bacon grease is more flavorsome for frying than cooking oils. Save it in a can with snug-fitting lid.

In bear country, don't store food in a convertible. A bear will go through the top as easily as though it were cheesecloth. Store food in the car trunk, hang it out of reach from a tree limb, or use "bear-proof," G.I.-surplus steel ammunition boxes. (These have waterproof gaskets, too.)

Rinsing a saucepan in cold water before scalding milk helps prevent sticking.

Use a light greasing on a cast-iron griddle for the first pancake. Then rub with a cut raw potato (peeled, of course) between batches. This will produce golden-brown flapjacks that won't stick.

For an efficient and inexpensive fire extinguisher, place an inch of rice in the bottom of a plastic detergent bottle (quart size, or smaller), then fill with bicarbonate of soda. (Rice absorbs moisture and prevents soda from caking.) Replace cap, drill this with a few ⅛-inch holes. If the camp stove flares up, squeeze the bottle and flying soda will extinguish the blaze immediately.

You can cut down grease greatly in camp food by frying meats in a fine dusting of salt in the skillet, instead of fat or shortening.

For camp stoves that must be primed with alcohol, use a plastic nasal spray bottle. Squeeze this, insert the nipple into the alcohol supply and release. This sucks in fuel. Aim the bottle at the priming pan and squeeze again. You'll get a fine stream that can be guided without spilling.

If the filter on the fuel funnel gets lost, use a piece of nylon stocking large enough to fill the funnel and overlap the edges. Hold in place with an elastic band.

Stew dried fruits during supper preparations. They'll then be ready for breakfast.

If a flour sifter is too bulky to fit in your kitchen box, take along a foot-square piece of aluminum screening. It can be rolled snugly and sifts flour, baking powder, soda, et cetera, beautifully.

Don't salt meats while (or before) they're being broiled. Salt starts juices running and you'll lose flavor.

A wire basket corn popper can be used for fireplace grilling of frankfurters, too.

If daytime temperature isn't enough to melt it, butter will keep surprisingly well if wrapped in waxed paper.

Fresh eggs will keep well if dipped quickly in melted paraffin.

Vegetables, such as celery, cabbage, radishes, and lettuce will keep fresh if wrapped in aluminum foil and then several layers of brown paper.

Slab bacon will keep without molding for long periods if first washed in water and small amount of soda, then dried over a smoky fire.

Some camping mothers with peanut-butter-and-jelly-sandwich loving children, premix the ingredients for the handy and quick "manufacturing" of sandwiches in camp or en route. The same can be done with peanut butter and marshmallow creams.

A camp-kitchen canister set can be made from ½-, 1-, 2-, and 4-pound coffee cans. Label each Tea, Coffee, Sugar, Flour, et cetera.

Chapter XXIII

Recipes

NOTE: Baking time and temperatures are suggested in some recipes for Coleman or similar ovens. All such recipes may also be baked in Dutch or reflector ovens, but exact time and temperature can't be stipulated for these.

ONE POT MEALS

Skillet Meal

1 pound ground beef
1 tablespoon cooking oil or margarine
1 6-ounce package noodles
1 can mixed peas and carrots
1 package onion soup mix

Sauté meat in oil or margarine until browned, then add onion soup mix and noodles, plus 2 cups of water. Cover and simmer 20 to 25 minutes. Spread peas and carrots over mixture and cook added 5 to 7 minutes. Serves six to eight.

Hungarian Camp Goulash

6 medium potatoes
1 pound Polish sausage
2 tablespoons bacon fat
2 onions
1 large can tomatoes

Peel and slice potatoes; boil in as little water as possible. Cut sausage into bite-size pieces and fry in bacon fat with onions until latter are light brown. Add tomatoes and simmer. When potatoes are done, add to meat-tomato mixture and stir. Season to taste. Serves four to six.

Sloppy Joes (Untidy Josephs among the genteel!)

1 pound ground beef
2 tablespoons prepared mustard
4 tablespoons catsup
1 can condensed chicken gumbo soup

Sauté hamburger until browned (onions may be added). Add other ingredients but do not dilute soup. Heat through and serve on hot, buttered hamburger rolls. A favorite among teen-agers. Serves six to eight.

Chinese Hash

1 pound hamburger
1 cup chopped onions
1 cup chopped celery
1 can mushroom soup
1 can cream of chicken soup
1 small can mushrooms
½ cup uncooked rice
¼ cup soy sauce
Dash of pepper
1 can Chow Mein noodles
1 can peas

Sauté hamburger, onions, and celery until vegetables are done. Then mix soups, mushrooms, rice, soy sauce, pepper, and ½ cup of water. Add to ground beef in 2-quart casserole. Bake covered in Coleman oven 30 minutes at 350 degrees. Uncover and bake 30 minutes more. During last 15 minutes, add peas and noodles. Serves six generously.

Budget Chop Suey

1 pound ground beef
3 large onions, sliced
1 teaspoon salt
½ teaspoon pepper
1 bunch celery, diced
2 green peppers, cut in strips
2 teaspoons sugar
2 cans bean sprouts
¼ cup cornstarch
4 teaspoons soy sauce

Combine ground beef, onions, salt and pepper, brown lightly in a little fat. Add celery, green pepper, 1½ cups hot water. Simmer 15 minutes. Add bean sprouts and thicken with cornstarch, sugar, and ¼ cup cold water. Cook uncovered 3 minutes. Add soy sauce and serve on rice or noodles. Serves six to eight generously.

Spaghetti with Bacon

2 pounds spaghetti
1 pound bacon
1 large onion, chopped
1 small green pepper
spaghetti sauce

Cook spaghetti as usual. Cut bacon into 1-inch pieces and fry. When almost done, add chopped onion and green pepper. Finish frying. Add 2 or 3 cans of your favorite spaghetti sauce. Many prefer to serve sauce separately, but it is easier to keep the meal hot if the sauce is mixed with spaghetti. French bread goes well with this dish. Serves eight.

Hamburger Stroganoff

2 pounds ground beef
½ teaspoon pepper
¼ cup shortening
⅓ cup chile sauce
1 cup chopped onion
1 clove garlic, minced
1½ cups sour cream
2 small cans sliced mushrooms, drained
2 teaspoons salt
¼ cup flour
1 teaspoon Worcestershire sauce

Brown meat, using half of shortening. Add remaining shortening, mushrooms, onion, garlic, salt and pepper. Sauté until onion is tender. Add Worcestershire sauce. Stir in flour, then chile sauce. Just before serving, blend in sour cream. Serve over hot noodles or spaghetti. Serves eight.

Top-of-Stove Casserole

1 can cream of mushroom soup
1 can whole green beans
1 bag potato chips

Heat soup with only half of water called for in directions. Add green beans and heat through. If dish is to be served at once, crumble potato chips over top and serve. If not, add other half of water (omitted from soup), cover with potato chips, and keep warm in oven not longer than 30 minutes. Cream of chicken or cheese soup may be used in place of mushroom soup. Serves two or three.

Chile Con Carne

1 can tomatoes	1 can red kidney beans
1 can corned beef	chile pepper
1 onion, chopped	

Mix tomatoes, corned beef, onion with dash of salt and pepper, and cook 30 minutes. Add beans and chile pepper to suit and cook additional 15 minutes. Serves four to six.

Antigonish

1 medium-size onion	2 eggs
1 medium-size can stewed tomatoes	pinch salt, pepper, basil

Chop onion and sauté in butter or margarine. When golden brown, add enough flour to make a paste. Add tomatoes and stir well. When bubbling starts, mix in two eggs, well beaten. Stir occasionally, season with salt, pepper, and a little basil. Remove from heat when thickened. Serves two to three on saltines.

Leftover Casserole

1 can cream of vegetable soup
1½ cups leftover turkey, pork, or chicken, cut into chunks

Add meat to soup and bake at 400 degrees for 20 minutes in Coleman oven. Serves 4 on toast or on rice.

Speedy Chicken Dinner

1 15½ ounce can boned chicken	3 celery stalks
	1 can peas
1 13 ounce can chicken broth	

Cut celery into small pieces and cook slowly in chicken broth. When done, thicken with a little flour, then add cut up chicken. Add peas and heat through. Serve over rice for four persons.

Quickie Pot Meal

1½ pounds ground beef	2 medium-size cans mixed

4 onions, sliced   peas and carrots
2 medium-size cans   6 potatoes, sliced thin
    tomatoes

Mix together meat, onions, tomatoes, peas and carrots, potatoes. Salt and pepper to suit. Add enough water so that liquid covers bottom of skillet or pot. Cover and cook about 10 minutes or until potatoes are done. Serves six to eight.

Pork Chop and Rice Dinner
4 pork chops or tenderloins   1 cup uncooked rice
1 onion, sliced   1 No. 2 can tomatoes

Wipe and salt chops or tenderloins. Trim off some fat if excessive. Lay on the bottom of Dutch oven or skillet, with large slice of onion over each piece of meat. Add rice, cover with tomatoes. Cover and cook 1 hour. Check occasionally to be sure there is enough liquid. If necessary, add a little water or, better still, liquid from tomatoes. Serves four.

Rice and Sausage
1 cup quick rice   1 pound pork sausage
1 can tomato soup

Cook sausage in patty form until almost done. Place about half of rice in greased tin, lay in sausage patties, then add rest of the rice. Mix the tomato soup with ¼ cup of sausage fat and pour over rice. Bake at 350 degrees for 40 minutes in Coleman oven. Serves four.

Peanut-Buttered Ham
1½ pounds canned ham,   ½ cup peanut butter
    Spam, Treat, Mor,   3 teaspoons mustard, dry
    or similar

Place 1-inch thick slices of meat in pan, spread peanut butter over each. Add dabs of mustard. Add water to ¼-inch depth. Bake 30 minutes before brisk reflector oven fire, or in Coleman oven at 350 degrees. Serves four.

Canadian Bacon

2 pounds Canadian Bacon
1 teaspoon dry mustard
½ cup brown sugar
1 cup pineapple juice

Spread meat with mixture of mustard and sugar. Place in baking tin, add pineapple juice and bake 45 minutes in reflector or Coleman oven. Serves eight.

Macaroni and Cheese with Vienna Sausage

2 cans macaroni and cheese   2 cans Vienna sausage

Slice sausage into bite-size bits. Add to macaroni and cheese, cook over slow heat until thoroughly heated. Stir often. It's inclined to stick! Serves six to eight.

Wieners in Tomatoes

1 pound frankfurters
1 No. 2 can tomatoes
4 tablespoons catsup
¼ cup butter or margarine
1 teaspoon salt

Cut frankfurters into bite-size pieces, lay in skillet. Cover with tomatoes and catsup combined. Dot with butter, sprinkle with salt, and cook until sauce is thick. Takes 20 to 30 minutes. Serves six to eight.

Franks Potato Salad

1 pound frankfurters
6 medium potatoes,
    sliced thin
1 teaspoon salt
2 tablespoons bacon fat
½ cup vinegar
1 onion, chopped

Lay potatoes in bottom of skillet and overlay with frankfurters cut to bite-size. Cover meat with remaining ingredients mixed together. Simmer gently 12 to 15 minutes. Serves six to eight.

Onions and Salt Pork

8 slices salt pork, ¼-inch
    thick
4 onions, sliced
3 tablespoons bacon fat

Place onions in skillet and cover with salt pork. Add 2 cups water and cook until water has boiled away. Add bacon fat and fry until pork is nicely browned. Serves four.

Liver Caucomgomoc

I first tasted this deep in the woods near Caucomgomoc Lake, Maine. We'd just shot a deer and my Border Patrol partner took charge of preparing the liver. Since then, I've used the same recipe with beef liver and it's almost as good.

1 pound beef liver	1 No. 2 can tomatoes
3 tablespoons shortening	1 large onion, chopped
¼ cup flour	Heavy sprinkling of pepper
1 teaspoon salt	

Sprinkle sliced liver with salt, pepper, and flour; brown in a skillet with fat. Mix tomatoes and onions, add to liver, cover and simmer slowly 25 minutes, or until liver is done. Serves four.

Chinese Rice-A-Roni

With the easy availability of Chinese food ingredients in most supermarkets, it's a simple matter to enjoy Oriental flavors in camp.

1 package Rice-A-Roni, either chicken or beef	1-pound can Chinese vegetables
	Soy sauce

Cook Rice-A-Roni according to directions. Add Chinese vegetables and soy sauce to taste. Heat thoroughly. Can be topped with Chinese noodles. Serves four to six.

Trapper's Toast

This is actually a trail dish for cold-morning breakfast, but it will serve nicely for a quick lunch.

¾ pound salt pork	Sliced bread
½ cup sugar	

Fry salt pork until all grease is drawn. Remove the pork, add sugar to fat, and stir until mixture is smooth. Remove most of this syrup into a cup. Fry bread in remaining mixture, adding to it from the cup as the bread is fried. Eat with fried salt pork. You can wrassle a catamount after this meal!

Meat Loaf

1 pound ground beef	1½ teaspoon salt
1 egg	1 onion
½ cup bread crumbs or crackers	4 strips bacon
	1 cup tomato juice or soup

Beat egg, mix all ingredients except bacon. Place in baking tin or in loaf form on aluminum foil, lay bacon strips on top, and bake before brisk fire in reflector oven about 50 minutes, or in Coleman oven. A raw, chopped, green pepper will add flavor. Serves six.

French-Canadian Tourtiere

Legend in my family has it that a cookee (a cook's helper, not a tidbit!) was killed when lumberjacks in my grandfather's Wisconsin lumbercamp stampeded into the cookhouse where my grandmother had baked "tourtiéres" —two-crust French-Canadian meat pies

1 pound ground beef (Gramma used venison)	1 teaspoon salt
1 onion, chopped	2 tablespoons catsup
1 tablespoon butter	1 box pie crust mix

Sauté onion in butter. Add ground meat and continue to sauté until meat starts to brown well, then add catsup and seasoning. Line pie plate with crust, pour in meat mixture while hot and lay on top crust, pinching edges and wetting as with fruit pie. Cut two or three slits in top crust. Place in Dutch, reflector, or Coleman oven and bake about 30 minutes, or until crust is browned. Like baked beans, the tourtiére's flavor improves with each warmover. Serves six to eight.

Pot Roast

This is a meal which requires considerably more than the one hour which I feel should limit most camp cooking However, once assembled, a pot roast requires little attention. It's a worthwhile exception to the rule.

4 pounds beef	2 onions
1 tablespoon flour	6 potatoes
4 carrots (or one can)	salt and pepper

Use a piece of chuck, rump, round, or shoulder. Sprinkle with salt, pepper, and flour. Brown in Dutch oven using a little fat if meat is very lean. Add enough water to cover bottom of kettle 1½ inches and simmer slowly 2½ hours or until meat is almost done. Then add vegetables, slicing or dicing potatoes. Continue slow simmering until done. Make a gravy of the broth with flour. Keep lid on kettle, but, if using Dutch oven, don't place coals on cover. Keep an eye on water level if barometer is dropping. Liquids evaporate quickly during a drop in barometric pressure! Serves eight to ten. Leftovers improve with reheating!

Weenie Wrap-ups

1 pound frankfurters	8 thin slices boiled ham
¼ pound cheddar cheese cut in strips	8 frankfurter rolls

Slit each frankfurter lengthwise. Insert strip of cheese, then wrap in slice of ham, fastening with toothpicks. Place on rack over glowing coals and roast. Baste frequently with glaze until browned. Serve in frankfurter rolls, toasted.

Glaze:

½ cup light corn syrup	½ teaspoon grated orange rind
2 teaspoons dry mustard	
3 tablespoons brown sugar	1 tablespoon butter or margarine

Combine all ingredients in small saucepan and heat until well blended. Serves two apiece to four campers.

Gourmet Hamburgers

2 pounds ground beef	1 tablespoon A-1 sauce
1 onion, chopped	¼ pound bleu cheese

Season meat with salt and pepper to suit, mix with chopped onion and A-1 sauce. Make 12 patties. Crumble bleu cheese over 6 of these and top with other 6. Press edges together. Grill over glowing coals. Turn once and cook until done. Serves six.

Woods Twist

Biscuit mix	Onion, sliced
Beef, ½- to ¾-inch thick, cut size of a quarter	

Slide slices of beef and onions, alternating, onto a stick of sweet wood such as maple. Mix thick biscuit dough and wrap around meat-onions on stick. Prop over fire on two forked sticks (making a miniature crane) and cook slowly, turning often. When done, pull out stick, add a dash of soy sauce.

Beef Kabobs

Cubes of chuck steak are placed on a stick, as described in Woods Twist, alternating with onion slices and squares of bacon. For variations, use wedges of tomato and green pepper, cubes of Swiss cheese, and sweet pickle slices. Cook as described in Woods Twist. A Boy and Girl Scout favorite, fun to cook, and even more fun to eat.

Shish-Kabobs

A true Shish-Kabob is made with lamb. Cut this into 1¼-inch cubes and alternate on a green stick or skewer with pimento, orange bits, and green pepper slices, or onions and whole mushrooms. Cook as described in Woods Twist, but omit covering of dough. For added flavor, marinate lamb cubes overnight or for several hours in sauce made from following:

1 cup vinegar
½ cup salad oil
¼ teaspoon garlic salt
¼ teaspoon salt

¼ teaspoon pepper
1 teaspoon flavoring salt
    or Savory salt

Hamburgers on a Stick

1 small can undiluted
    evaporated milk
1 egg
1½ pounds ground beef
½ cup fine cracker crumbs
1½ teaspoons salt

¼ teaspoon pepper
1 teaspoon onion flakes
½ green pepper, chopped
24 slices tomato (small
    and firm)
12 onion slices

Mix milk, egg, beef, crumbs, salt, pepper, onion flakes, and green pepper. Make 24 small meat balls. Slide these carefully on to stick of sweet wood or skewer, alternating meat balls, onion slices, and tomato slices. Broil 5 minutes, turning frequently. Serves six.

Angels on Horseback

A Girl Scout specialty, popular with older children in family camping.

1 pound cheese
16 slices bacon

8 split rolls
Lettuce

Cut cheese into 1-inch cubes. Wrap with bacon. Bacon is best handled if pan-broiled until about half-done before wrapping it around cheese. Insert toothpick to hold. Run a sharp stick through it and toast quickly over fire. Have a split roll ready, lined with lettuce, to hold the "angel" when it's ready to "unhorse," or if it seems ready to fall off the stick.

Camper's Stew

If you want to disregard the one-hour limit on food preparation time in camp, a camper's stew is a rewarding violation of a rule! It may be prepared in any kind of a kettle, even a tin-can tea pail, but a Dutch oven or similar iron pot will impart a flavor unmatched by any other utensil. Cooks, bent upon building a stew, usually clean out the larder. Ingredients, therefore, vary greatly but the following recipe is typical:

3 pounds lean beef	1 tomato
½ pound salt pork	1 cup carrots
4 onions	¼ cup flour
1 cup peas	2 teaspoons salt
½ cup instant rice	1 cup soaked lima beans
1 cup whole kernel corn	

Cut meat into 1-inch cubes. Chop salt pork into small pieces and start to fry in Dutch oven. When there's enough fat, add chopped onions (or sliced) and cook until they start to soften noticeably. Add meat and brown. Then, add 4 to 6 quarts of water and simmer slowly for about 2 hours. The secret to a tasty stew is slow simmering, so that it bubbles lazily. Add lima beans. Simmer another ½ hour. Add potatoes and vegetables if latter are fresh. If canned vegetables are used, add when potatoes are done, along with minute rice. Continue simmering until all are heated through. This recipe will feed six amply, but if you make a double batch, the leftovers will improve with each heating. Broth may be thickened with flour.

Minuteman Mulligan

2 cans cream of celery soup	2 teaspoons salt
2 pounds ground meat	2 tablespoons shortening
1 cup fine bread crumbs	3 tablespoons pickle relish
1 egg	1 pepper, chopped

Blend soup with half the water recommended in directions. Measure out ¼ cup of this mixture, combine with meat, bread crumbs, egg, onion, pepper, and salt. Shape into balls about 1 inch in diameter. Brown in skillet in shortening. Add remaining soup and relish. Cover and cook over low heat 20 minutes, stirring often. Serves eight.

Coffee-Can Stew

Here's a clever idea for supper on the first night in camp when everyone, including the cook, is tired from a long day's drive.

1½ pounds ground beef	6 stalks celery
3 carrots	3 medium onions
3 medium potatoes	1 large green pepper,
3 medium tomatoes	chopped
salt and pepper	3 vacuum-type coffee cans
6 strips bacon	with lids

Just before departure from home, or night before: Make 6 patties of ground meat. Cut bacon slices in half; cut carrots lengthwise, then in half; chop celery coarsely. Slice onions, potatoes, and tomato. Put 2 strips of bacon in bottom of each can, over which place slices of onion, meat patty, more onion, a layer of potato, green pepper, celery, carrots—then a second patty, vegetables over this and top with 2 strips of bacon. If can is not full, fill space with crumpled wax paper. Seal can with masking tape and place in camp ice chest.

Upon arrival at camp: Remove seal and wax paper, replace cover, and place cans on hot coals or over low camp-stove flame. After ten minutes, check. If browning too fast, add 2 tablespoons water. Replace lid and cook 15 minutes. Serves six (two to a can).

Dot's Camp Stew

I haven't the slightest idea who Dot is, but her clever idea for a camp stew produces a delicious meal for five or six persons.

2 cans corned or roast beef	2 large onions
6 medium potatoes	5 carrots, sliced thin

Slice vegetables into pan of cold water. Allow to stand while meat is prepared. Place contents of each can on a sheet of heavy-duty aluminum foil, season to taste. Pile half of vegetables on each meat loaf, dot with butter, season with salt and pepper. Wrap each loaf carefully so juices cannot escape. Place over coals. Cook one hour. You get a bonus with this stew: No dishes to wash!

Meatless Stew

2 medium-size onions, sliced	¼ cup shortening or bacon fat
1 No. 2 can tomatoes	salt and pepper
1 green pepper, chopped	
8 eggs	

Sauté onions in shortening. Add tomatoes and peppers; cook 30 minutes. Break in eggs and when these are cooked firm, or to suit, serve on toast or crackers. Serves four.

Hot Dog Stew

½ cup chopped onions	5 large potatoes, diced
2 tablespoons bacon fat	1 pound frankfurters, sliced thin

Sauté onions in fat, add potatoes and frankfurters. Add just enough water to prevent scorching. Cover and simmer until potatoes are done. A tossed salad goes well with this. Serves four to six.

If You Hash Me

This one is named in honor of the most infamous pun I ever heard. I'd cooked the hash for a fisherman I was guiding and he must have been verging on starvation. He liked it. His comment was "If you hash me, this is the best ..." His jokes were so bad I charged him a little extra.

1 pound minced ham	1 can corned beef
3 cold boiled potatoes	1 can condensed vegetable soup
2 tablespoons bacon fat	1 onion, chopped

Sauté meat loosely in fat. Add potato, onion, and corned beef, chopped fine. Mix well and stir frequently. Add undiluted vegetable soup and continue heating until done. I like mine slightly crisp around the edges. Serves four to six.

Hash Rolls

Roll a biscuit dough (made from prepared mix) about ½-inch thick. Spread hash over dough and then roll into a snug cylinder. Slice about ¾-inch thick and fry in bacon fat until browned.

Green Mountain Chowder

¼ cup chopped onions   1 can tuna
1 can condensed cream of
         vegetable soup

Sauté onions in fat until tender but not browned. Blend in soup with ¾ can of water. Drain and flake tuna. Add to chowder. Stir and heat until very hot. Season to suit. Serves five or six.

NEFCA Corn Chowder

4 strips bacon   2 cups diced raw potatoes
2 cups cream-style corn   salt and pepper
      (1 pound can)   2 cups milk
1 medium onion, sliced   1 tablespoon butter
      thin

Cook bacon in saucepan until some of fat is "tried out." Add onion and cook until bacon is crisp and onion is slightly browned. Remove bacon and drain on absorbent paper. Add 2 cups water and diced potatoes with salt and pepper to suit. Simmer covered about 20 minutes. Add milk and simmer 5 minutes more. Just before serving, add butter, and bacon crumbled into bits. Serves six.

Potato Mix Chowder

1 box scalloped potato mix   1 can mixed vegetables
3 cups milk   ½ pound frankfurters

To scalloped potato mix, add 3 cups of water and cook 10 minutes. Add milk and mixed vegetables. Cook 5 minutes more. Slice and brown frankfurters, then add these. Simmer slowly until thoroughly heated, then sprinkle with grated sharp cheddar cheese. Serves four.

Logger's Onion Chowder

½ pound salt pork, sliced ¼-inch thick	6 potatoes
	milk
6 medium onions, sliced	

"Try out" salt pork in chowder kettle, and when nearly done, add onions. Sauté these until browned, then add potatoes plus enough water to cover. Simmer until potatoes are done. Add milk to desired consistency (some like this chowder thick—others thin). Bring to boiling point, remove from heat, salt and pepper to suit. Serves four.

Succotash Chowder

½ pound salt pork, sliced (or bacon)	1 can lima beans
	½ pint milk
1 onion, chopped	salt and pepper
1 can cream-style corn	

"Try out" salt pork or bacon. Remove and pour out about half of fat. Sauté onions until lightly browned. Add corn, beans, milk, salt and pepper to suit. Simmer gently until very hot. Crumple salt pork or bacon on top and serve. Serves four.

Fish Chowder

Almost any fish can be used for chowder, of course, but I prefer trout—small ones. New Yorkers often add tomatoes, but otherwise they're usually pretty nice folks.

2 pounds fish	2 teaspoons salt
6 slices bacon, diced	dash of pepper
2 small onions, chopped coarsely	1 quart milk

Simmer fish in slightly salted water until meat can be separated from bones easily. Save the water but drain off bits of skin, bone, et cetera. Fry bacon and onion together until browned. Add potatoes to water in which fish was cooked, plus salt and pepper. When potatoes are done, add fish, bacon, onions, and milk. Bring to a boil but don't boil! Use minimum amount of water for cooking fish and potatoes. Serves six.

Corned Beef Vegetable Soup

1 can corned beef	1 teaspoon parsley flakes
6 medium potatoes, diced	1 teaspoon celery flakes
1 bunch carrots	1 teaspoon sweet pepper
1 medium onion, chopped coarsely	flakes

Mix potatoes, carrots, onions, add seasonings. Break corned beef into small chunks and add to vegetables with Worcestershire sauce. Cover with water and simmer until vegetables are done, usually about 1 hour. A pressure cooker will do the job in 10 to 15 minutes. Serves four to six.

Easy Onion Soup

3 large onions, sliced	4 tablespoons butter
2 cans beef bouillon or consommé	

Brown onions slightly in butter. Add to bouillon and simmer until onions are tender. Season to suit. Sprinkle with grated cheese when serving. Serves four or five.

Hasty Vegetable Soup

2 cans mixed vegetables	salt and pepper
2 cans beef bouillon or consommé	

Mix vegetables, bouillon, 4 cups of water and simmer 10 minutes. Serves six.

Crisp Croutons

These add a nice touch to soups. Cube day-old bread. Melt 2 tablespoons of butter in skillet, toss in bread cubes, sprinkle with onion or garlic salt. Fry until brown and crisp. Serve on soup.

Souplings

Especially tasty with tomato or chicken soup. Moisten biscuit mix with enough milk or water to make a dough that can be molded into 1-inch balls. Insert a cube of cheese into balls and drop into simmering soup for about 3 minutes, or until cooked through.

Baked Beans in a Hurry

4 slices bacon	¼ teaspoon salt
1 onion, chopped	¼ teaspoon dry mustard
1 tablespoon molasses	1½ tablespoon catsup
1 medium-sized can baked beans	

Fry bacon until crisp, then remove strips. Sauté onion in fat, add molasses, salt, mustard, catsup, and beans, mixing thoroughly. Sprinkle crumpled bacon on top. Bake 15 minutes and no one will believe they're canned beans! Serves two to three.

Beans and Meat Balls

1 pound ground beef	1 tablespoon hot shortening
½ cup evaporated milk	1 cup sliced onions
⅔ cup soft bread crumbs	1 pound can baked beans
1⅛ teaspoon salt	(2 cups)
¼ teaspoon pepper	2 tablespoons catsup
	¼ teaspoon dry mustard

Mix well ground beef, evaporated milk, bread crumbs, 1 teaspoon salt, and pepper. Wet hands and shape mixture into 16 meat balls. Brown in skillet in shortening with onions. Cover and cook over low heat 10 minutes. Add mixture of beans, ⅛ teaspoon salt, catsup, and dry mustard. Cover and heat. Serves four.

Cheese-Bean Hot Sandwich

1-pound can of baked beans	1 tablespoon chopped
3 tablespoons chile sauce	sweet pickle

Heat beans with chile sauce and pickle. Top generously

with shredded sharp cheddar cheese. Serve on hot buttered buns. Serves four.

Apple Bean Dandy

1 No. 2 can baked beans	5 slices bacon
1 apple, chopped fine	¼ cup brown sugar

Place half of the baked beans in greased baking tin and sprinkle with half of the sugar and apple. Add balance of beans, sprinkle with remaining apple and sugar. "Try out" bacon until half done. Pour fat over beans, lay slices of bacon on top and bake at 325 degrees for 25 minutes. Serves two to four.

Hearty Bean Salad

Garlic salt	½ pound cheddar cheese
2 1-pound cans red kidney beans	2 cups celery, diced
	1 cup carrots, grated
lettuce	French dressing
½ cup red pepper relish	

Sprinkle garlic salt over beans. Line a bowl with crisp lettuce and sprinkle with red pepper relish. Cube cheddar cheese and place in center of bowl; surround with celery and carrots. Add beans. Toss with your favorite French dressing. This is an ideal meal for one of those hot days in camp when eating seems a strenuous effort. Serves eight.

VEGETABLES

Tom's Treat Potatoes

Dice 4 cold cooked potatoes and 6 strips of bacon. Fry bacon until crisp, pour off half the fat. Fry potatoes with sliced onions in remaining fat until lightly browned. Then break in 4 eggs, salt and pepper to suit and stir lightly until eggs are set. Sprinkle with bacon. Serves four.

Camp-fried Potatoes

¼ pound bacon	6 medium potatoes, sliced
2 onions, sliced	

Fry bacon until crisp; add onions and fry until about half cooked. Add potatoes, season with salt and pepper. Cook slowly with cover on skillet until potatoes are soft. Remove cover, turn up heat, and brown potatoes quickly. Serves three to four.

Tasty Taters
Pare and cut potato into 6 pieces. Sprinkle with dry onion soup mix; add 1 teaspoon water and dab of butter. Seal in heavy-duty aluminum foil. Bake 20 minutes on hot coals or slightly longer on fireplace grill.

SAUCES

White Sauce Mix
This white sauce may be "pre-fabricated" in quantity for use in camp simply by adding water. Sift and measure 1½ cups of flour. Add 1 tablespoon salt, ¼ teaspoon pepper. Put in dry plastic bag or strong brown paper bag. Add 1 pound non-fat dry milk. Holding top of bag tightly, shake for a minute to mix thoroughly. Store in jar or canister.

To make white sauce in camp: Measure water and mix to make desired amount and kind of sauce. Put mix in pan, add ⅓ cup water to moisten and stir. Add remaining water. Heat and stir constantly until thickened. For extra richness, add 2 tablespoons butter or margarine for each cup of sauce.

For thin white sauce:
⅓ cup mix and 1 cup water.

For medium white sauce:
½ cup mix and 1 cup water.

For thick white sauce:
⅔ cup mix and 1 cup water.

Barbecue Sauce
½ cup catsup   1½ teaspoon brown sugar
1 teaspoon horseradish   few drops olive oil

Mix as listed above. Apply to chicken or hamburger with pastry brush or a new 1-inch paint brush.

Button Bay Barbecue Sauce

1 10½-ounce can condensed tomato soup
¼ cup sweet pickle relish
¼ cup chopped onion
1 tablespoon vinegar or lemon juice

Combine ingredients, cover, and simmer 5 to 10 minutes, or until onion is cooked and flavors are blended. Makes 1½ cups. Serve over chicken, franks, or burgers.

Hula Ham Sauce

¼ cup brown sugar
1 tablespoon dry mustard
2 tablespoons powdered ginger
⅛ teaspoon garlic powder
1 tablespoon soy sauce
1 tablespoon lemon juice

Combine and stir until smooth, then add one cup pineapple juice. Baste broiling ham with this sauce for a special delicacy.

Ten Minute Spaghetti-Meat Sauce

The secret of getting a good spaghetti sauce in 10 minutes of course, is the pressure cooker.

2 tablespoons salad oil
1 pound ground beef
2 large onions, sliced
2 8-ounce cans tomato sauce
1 6-ounce can tomato paste
2 to 3 teaspoons chili powder
1 teaspoon salt
1 teaspoon sugar
dash red pepper

Combine all ingredients in pressure cooker. ½ cup of water may be included. Cook at 15-pound pressure for 10 minutes. Reduce pressure at once. Serve over cooked spaghetti with grated parmesan cheese.

Fish Sauce
    ½ cup butter   ¼ cup lemon juice
    2 egg yolks

    Combine egg yolks, lemon juice and half of butter in double boiler and heat until butter is melted. Add balance of butter and cook until sauce is thickened. Stir well.

Onion-Bacon Gravy
    Use bacon fat for making this tasty gravy. For each ½ cup of bacon grease, add ½ cup flour. Stir until flour is well browned. Add 4 cups milk and 2 tablespoons dehydrated onion flakes. Cook until gravy is smooth and season with salt and pepper to taste.

Brown Sugar Syrup
    If you run out of maple syrup for pancakes some morning, melt brown sugar in small amount of water, simmering it until it clarifies. A few drops of maple flavoring or a dash of extract may be added.

BREAKFASTS

Variations on a Pancake
    Pancake mixes produce good flapjacks but interesting variations are possible:

    Add a little butter and an egg to the batter to make them richer.
    Or a few bits of finely chopped apple and a dash of sugar and cinnamon.
    Or bits of crisp bacon and ⅓ cup of grated cheese.
    Or fresh-picked blueberries or a cup of canned (drained) blueberries.
    Seedless raisins become "nice and fluffy" in pancakes.
    If butter or syrup is in short supply, top flapjacks witn a tart jelly.

Corn Pancakes
    Mix a package of corn muffin mix according to directions. Set aside for 10 minutes or so. Drop by the spoonful

on a hot griddle and cook as you would a regular pancake batter. Serve with butter or syrup.

Floaters

Nothing more than delicious pancakes! One of the guides with whom I used to work was prone to praising his own handiwork over a cook fire. "These are so light, they'll float away . . ." he used to brag about his flapjacks. We called them "floaters" but they *were* good!

1 cup flour	¼ teaspoon salt
1 teaspoon soda	1 egg
1 teaspoon baking powder	1½ cups sour milk
1 tablespoon butter	

Mix dry ingredients. Add milk, egg (beaten) and butter (melted). Use minimum stirring to blend and don't try to beat out the lumps. Leave them in. Cook on medium-heated griddle or skillet. Serves two to three.

Cream of Tartar Flapjacks

1½ cups flour	milk
2 teaspoons cream of tartar	1 egg
¼ teaspoon salt	2 tablespoons butter
1 teaspoon soda	3 tablespoons sugar

Combine dry ingredients; add beaten egg and enough milk to form thin batter. Add melted butter and beat slowly and gently. Fry on griddle or in skillet. Serves four.

Corn Fritters

In some quarters these are not considered breakfast food, but that's the time of day when I like them best.

1 can whole kernel corn	1¼ cups flour
2 teaspoons baking powder	1 teaspoon salt
⅓ cup milk	2 tablespoons butter
2 eggs, beaten	

Sift dry ingredients together. Add corn (including liquid), melted butter, egg, and enough milk to form a batter that will pour easily from a pitcher. Fry on hot griddle or in skillet. Incidentally, you'll make better pancakes if you keep them small—4 inches or less in diameter.

Rice-Poached Eggs

1½ cups minute rice	4 eggs
salt and pepper	1 tablespoon butter

Cook rice according to directions. When nearly done, press four depressions into it. Break an egg into each one, add salt and pepper lightly and a dab of butter. Cover and cook a few minutes or until eggs are set the way you like them. Serves four.

Trail Bacon

Cut ¼-inch slices from slab bacon. Soak in milk about ½ hour. Roll in flour and fry in skillet. This is the shortest recipe in the book, but it suggests one of the best cold-morning breakfasts I know of—especially if the coffee is good!

Eggs à la Round-up

This is not a cowboy recipe. It came from a Girl Scout who'd just returned from the Girl Scout Round-up at Button Bay, Vermont.

4 eggs	½ can condensed cream
4 tablespoons milk	of mushroom soup

Beat eggs and combine in frying pan with milk and undiluted soup. Scramble as with regular eggs. Season to suit. Serves two to three.

Skillet Toast

If you're having bacon for breakfast, don't throw out the fat. Fry a few pieces of bread in it, top with jelly and bacon. Hot coffee completes a fine breakfast.

Necessity Prunes

I once worked for a summer camp director who insisted that prunes are necessary to health. We had them *every* morning all season long! I later learned to disguise them once in a while. To 1 pound of prunes, add a No. 2 can of grapefruit juice and 3 tablespoons sugar. Simmer 30 minutes. Best made the night before and served at breakfast.

BREADS

Pineapple Bannock

biscuit mix	1 can pineapple chunks
1 egg	⅓ cup sugar
1 teaspoon cinnamon	

Use pineapple liquid in place of milk or water to make biscuit dough. Beat and add egg. Pour into greased tin, sprinkle with cinnamon, overlay with pineapple chunks. Bake 25 minutes in reflector or Coleman oven.

Saleratus Biscuits

"Saleratus" was a colonial, coarse-grained baking soda. It is no longer available as such, but the following recipe approximates a favorite of the old-time lumbercamp where the cook turned out Saleratus biscuits by the gross in his cookhouse stove. When spring came, he produced them in quantity in a 4-foot reflector "baker" to feed the "river pigs" as they hustled the logs along thaw-swollen rivers to the mills. Sometimes, a "cookee," the cook's helper, mixed the ingredients and heaven help him if he included too much saleratus. If the cook didn't do it first, the crew tossed him in among the logs!

2 cups flour	½ teaspoon salt
1 teaspoon cream of tartar	lard "the size of an egg"
½ teaspoon baking soda	1 cup milk

Mix the dry ingredients and blend in the lard; add milk until dough is sticky. Roll out and cut on floured board, or drop "blobs" of dough onto greased baking sheet. Lard is specified as the grease in old-time recipes but modern cooks are more likely to use shortening. Bake until brown, or until biscuits pass toothpick test. This recipe is especially suitable for reflector oven baking.

Baking Powder Biscuits

2 cups flour	1 teaspoon salt
4 teaspoons baking powder	1 cup milk
4 tablespoons shortening	

Mix flour, baking powder, milk, and salt; add shortening, blending in well until easily handled dough is attained. Roll out on floured pastry board (or canoe bottom) and cut into ½-inch-thick and 3-inch-square pieces. Bake 15 to 20 minutes in reflector oven before brisk hardwood fire or, at 400 degrees in Coleman oven. "Luxuriate" by splitting, buttering, and topping with canned fruit.

Pre-Fab Biscuits

Make the following mix in quantity before going on a camping trip:

8 cups all purpose flour	2 teaspoons cream of tartar
2 teaspoons salt	2 teaspoons sugar
16 teaspoons baking powder	2 cups shortening

Sift flour, salt, baking powder, cream of tartar, and sugar. Cut in shortening until mixture resembles coarse crumbs. Pack in coffee-can canister. When making biscuits in camp, add ½ to ¾ cup of milk to 2 cups mix. Can be baked in covered frying pan, on a stick, or in Coleman oven.

Variations on a Muffin

To the batter for one dozen muffins, whether made from a mix or from your own recipe, you can add one of the following combinations for a change in flavor:

A cup of washed and drained fresh blueberries—or the canned variety, also drained.

¼ cup of peanut butter thinned with a little milk.

A cup of raisins.

A square of baker's chocolate melted with one tablespoon butter and stirred into batter.

½ cup chopped dates.

2 cups whole kernel corn, canned or fresh.
A cup raw cranberries mixed with ½ cup sugar.

Jonnycake

2 cups yellow corn meal	2 eggs, well beaten
1½ cups flour	4 tablespoons shortening
1 teaspoon baking powder	1½ cups milk
large pinch salt	
1 teaspoon baking soda	

Mix all dry ingredients well. Blend in eggs, milk, and melted shortening and add to dry ingredients with minimum of stirring. Pour into shallow greased tin and bake 25 minutes at 375 degrees.

Sweet Corn Cake

¾ cup flour	1 egg
1 can whole kernel corn	1 teaspoon soda
¼ teaspoon salt	3 tablespoons sugar
2 teaspoons cream of tartar	milk

Mix all ingredients with enough milk to make a fairly thin batter. Pour into shallow greased tin and bake 25 minutes at 375 degrees.

HOT BEVERAGES

Guide's Coffee

You'll need 1 tablespoonful of regular-grind, high-grade, fresh coffee for each cup, plus, when I make it, a couple extra spoonfuls for the pot. Stir one egg into the coffee, shell and all, until the egg is thoroughly mixed in and the coffee moist. If timing is correct, the pot will have reached a vigorous boil at this point. Dump the coffee into the boiling water and allow it to "roll" gently for a minute or so—no longer! Then set the pot back away from heat, which might cause it to boil again, and dash in a cup of cold water. This settles the grounds so well that I've never repaired the screen in my pot's pouring spout. Your coffee will take on the color of fine old mahogany, and campers will be attracted by its aroma from as far as a quarter-mile away! The prime shortcoming of this coffee-making method is that a small quantity is difficult to brew, but you'll have little trouble disposing of 16 cups.

Quick Camp Coffee

Half the fun of drinking good coffee is the tantalizing wait while it brews, but here's a get-it-quick method for those in a hurry, (if you like cream and sugar in yours). Premix 1 part instant coffee, 1 part sugar and 1 part dried cream, in proportions you like. Pack this at home in a canister of some sort. At camp, you merely add boiling water to 3 teaspoons of the mixture per cup. Next step: An instant pill substitute for instant coffee!

Woodsman's Cocoa

Mix ½ cup sugar with 4 tablespoons cocoa. Add enough milk to form a heavy paste and stir until smooth. Mix one can evaporated milk with 1 quart boiling water. Add cocoa paste to this and bring back to a boil. Drink hot.

Woods Tea

Bring water to a vigorous boil in tea pail or kettle. There's no law against using your cook-kit coffee pot. For each cup of tea, add 1 level teaspoon bulk tea plus another for the pot. Remove kettle from fire immediately, but set it where it will keep hot. Put on lid and allow it to "steep" 5 minutes. Never steep tea any longer than this. If you want weaker tea, use more water; stronger tea, more tea. Most woods tea is drunk "straight," but there's no harm in adding a tiny dash of lemon juice or even sugar and cream, if you like.

MISCELLANEOUS ADDENDA

When Eleanor proofread the manuscript she thought that "miscellaneous addenda" sounded like an unattractive recipe. Her cooking is good; her jokes bad. The fact is that recipes have continued to pour in from campers even as this book was being completed. The following arrived and were tested too late to be "classified" in their correct categories.

Welsh Rarebit
- 1 can condensed cream of mushroom soup
- ½ cup milk
- 1 can tuna, chopped
- ¼ teaspoon oregano
- ½ teaspoon dry mustard
- 1 tablespoon Worcestershire sauce
- 1 small can pimentos, chopped
- ½ pound Velveeta cheese, shredded

Mix in 2-quart saucepan. Heat thoroughly until well blended, stirring frequently. Serve on saltines for four.

Golden Rarebit
Add a dash of mustard and enough milk to a can of cheddar cheese soup to make it the consistency of sauce. Serve over toast or crackers with several strips of crisp bacon.

Western Sandwich
- 4 eggs
- ¼ green pepper, chopped
- salt and pepper
- onion flakes
- 2 tablespoons butter, melted

Combine eggs, beaten slightly, with onion flakes or minced onions, green pepper, and turn into skillet in which butter has been melted. Salt and pepper to taste. Cook over low heat until eggs are firm. Cut into wedges and serve between slices of bread. Serves four.

Tuna Pot Pie
- 2 cans tuna (7-ounce size)
- 1 cup cooked, diced carrots
- 1 cup cooked peas
- 1 can condensed chicken soup
- 1 cup biscuit mix

Drain tuna and break into pieces. Combine carrots, peas, and tuna. Place in greased casserole or tin. Combine soup with ½ cup water and heat. Pour over tuna mixture. Prepare biscuit mix according to directions. Drop by spoonful over tuna. Bake in very hot oven, 450 degrees for 30 minutes, or until browned. Serves six.

Boiled Maine Lobster

Plunge live lobsters headfirst into 3 quarts boiling salted water. Cover and return to boiling point. Simmer 20 minutes. Drain. Place lobster on its back. With a sharp knife cut in half lengthwise. Remove the stomach, just back of the head, and the intestinal vein which runs from the stomach to the tip of the tail. Don't discard the green liver. This is the "tomalley" in Maine and a prized delicacy. Crack claws and pry out meat. Serve with drawn butter into which meat is dipped before eating. (The Department of Sea and Shore Fisheries, Augusta, Maine, issues a free instructional booklet for eating lobster!)

Apple in Hand

This is a dessert that youngsters will carry away from the table eagerly. They find it difficult to wait while adults dawdle over regular dessert. Make these up for them and send them on their way happily. Core whole apples. Mix peanut butter, either smooth or crunch-style, with raisins. Stuff mixture into holes in apples. Children like them whole, but they may also be sliced for "table serving."

Candy Bar Dessert

Spread peanut butter thinly over 12 graham crackers. Remove outer wrapper from 2 chocolate bars but do not remove inside wrapper. Place in cold frying pan and heat slowly until chocolate is soft enough to spread over the peanut-buttered crackers. Place second cracker on top and it's ready to eat, or more likely, gobble!

Some-Mores

Famous ever since the Girl Scouts were founded! For each serving you'll need:

4 squares thin milk chocolate
2 graham crackers
1 marshmallow

Toast marshmallow until browned. Place chocolate on graham cracker, then toasted marshmallow and cover with second cracker. They're a gooey mess, but delightful!

Fruit Cobbler

Prepare biscuit mix according to directions for making biscuits. Pat into an oblong on two thicknesses of aluminum foil. Spread ½ can of fruit pie filling (any kind will do), fold over, seal, and prick. Wrap completely in foil and bake on hot coals 7 minutes to a side (more or less!) Serve with cream.

Banana Shortcake

¼ cup butter	¼ teaspoon cinnamon
2 or 3 green-tipped bananas, peeled and quartered	¾ cup brown sugar
	4 1-inch slices pound cake
2 tablespoons lemon juice	

Melt butter in foilware pan, over coals. Add bananas and sprinkle with lemon juice, brown sugar, and cinnamon. Spoon liquid over bananas occasionally. Meanwhile, toast slices of pound cake over grill—(both sides of cake). Place bananas on cake and serve with topping.

Appendix

COOKING DEFINITIONS

Barbecue: The cooking of meat, fish, or poultry over coals or fire, on or in a grill or spit.

Baste: To spoon natural food juices or additional liquid over cooking food for added flavor or to prevent scorching.

Batter: A mixture, usually of flour and liquid such as water or milk and other ingredients.

Beat: Rapid, usually circular, strokes with a spoon or other implement to introduce air into a mixture of food and to mix ingredients.

Blanch: A preliminary cooking, usually in boiling water, for no more than 5 minutes for removing outer skin. May be followed by immersion in cold water to arrest cooking.

Braise: The cooking of meat by searing in small quantity of fat, then simmering in a covered dish. Generally used for tough cuts of meat.

Bread: Food is breaded when it is dipped into a liquid then into coarsely ground bread crumbs, usually prior to frying.

Broil: The cooking of food, usually meat, fish, or fowl, by direct radiant heat from coals or flames.

Clarify: To make liquids completely transparent. This is often done by adding egg white which, after heating, solidifies and collects foreign matter which may then be removed.

Cream Shortening: The stirring of shortening and the addition of small quantities of sugar until a smooth and fluffy texture is attained.

Cut In: By use of a knife, spoon, or even fingers, shortening is "cut into" flour until absorbed.

Deep Frying: To fry so that foods are immersed in hot fat.

Dredge: To coat with flour.

Drippings: Natural fats or juices which drip from cooking meats during broiling or which are cooked out while frying.

Fold: The mixing of one ingredient into another gently.

Fricassee: To stew or braise in a sauce or gravy.

Knead: The folding, refolding and turning of heavy dough, usually with the hands.

Marinate: Soaking food in liquid, generally a seasoned oil, to tenderize or add flavor.

Mince: Chopping food into fine particles.

Pan Broil: To cook, usually in a skillet, without fat or with just enough to prevent burning or sticking.

Parboil: Partial cooking in boiling water.

Poach: Cooking foods in liquid so that food is not dissolved or absorbed into liquid.

Preheat: Bringing oven or utensil to desired temperature before putting in food.

Puree: The straining of cooked food through a food sieve or strainer.

Render: Cooking solid fat until it is melted.

Rice: To force food through a ricer so that it takes on texture not unlike that of cooked rice.

Saute: To fry in small quantity of fat. Browning slightly.

Scald (milk): The heating of milk, usually in a double boiler, until a skim forms.

Scallop: Baking food in sauce, usually in a casserole.

Score: To cut slight indentations in surface of food with a knife or similar implement.

Sift: To combine dry ingredients through a strainer.

Simmer: Cooking in a liquid at slightly below boiling point. Surface of liquid should not bubble violently.

Skewer: To impale meat or other food on metal or wood shafts for cooking.

Skim: Removing fat or other substances that float atop a liquid.

Steam: To cook by means of steam arising from boiling water, the latter not directly in contact with the food.

Steep: Usually applicable to tea. Allowing tea leaves to stand in water below boiling point.

Stew: Same as Simmer.

MEASUREMENTS

I've known camp cooks, particularly on logging jobs where bread is baked by the dozen and doughnuts fried by the gross, who never used a measuring cup. They literally used "at lot o' this 'n a lotta that. . . ." When cooking in such quantities, an error of a half cup of flour makes little difference in the consumption rate of grub placed on the table that day. However, in family camp cooking, where quantities are more limited, accuracy of measurements takes on more importance. Not that you must bind yourself to 1/10 grain accuracy but you don't have the leeway of the lumberjack cook!

As a rule, when a recipe calls for teaspoon or tablespoon measurement, a level filling of the spoon is called for. Much the same is true of measuring cups.

If measurements call for a cupful of such ingredients as shortening or brown sugar, pack these into the cup well, leveling them off with a knife. One of the old camp cook tricks for measuring a half cup of grease calls for filling the cup half full of water, then adding the grease until the water level rises to a full cup. This is particularly handy when shortening is hard and difficult to pack into the cup. You have only to pour off the water and you have an accurate half cup of shortening!

Many cooks don't bother using a regular measuring cup, preferring a regular drinking cup which is included in the cook kit. This may not be exactly the same size as a standard measure, so it's a wise plan to check it out.

Cookbooks vary slightly in their opinions as to the temperature of a "hot" or "very hot" oven. Actually, a variance of 25 to 50 degrees isn't always critical so that, even with a Coleman oven and its temperature indicator, some degree of "by guess an' by gosh" is involved in baking or roasting. Dutch ovens and reflectors turn out masterpieces in the hands of skilled cooks who, most of the time, haven't the remotest conception of the actual heat in their ovens! The following chart should help a little, however:

Oven Temperature Guide

Very slow	250	degrees
Slow	300	"
Moderate slow	325	"
Moderate	350	"
Moderate hot	375	"
Hot	400	"
Very hot	450–500	"

COOKING AT HIGH ALTITUDE

Water boils at 212 degrees—at sea level. However, for each additional 600 feet of altitude, it boils at 1 degree lower. In other words, at 6,000 feet, the temperature of boiling water is roughly 10 degrees lower than at sea level. This will slow the cooking of certain foods, particularly the various vegetables that are cooked in water. However, this doesn't present the serious problems that it would seem to. You'll simply have to cook them a little longer. Several tables have been devised, arbitrarily indicating boiling time at various altitudes, but these are rarely accurate.

Baking at high altitude is another matter, particularly above 5,000 feet. A sound rule to follow is to decrease baking powder content by about 10 per cent for every 1,000 feet of altitude. Otherwise, you'll get cakes and biscuits with "big heads"—literally!

The Colorado Agricultural Station, Colorado A & M College at Fort Collins, Colorado, has done notable research in high altitude cooking and offers useful and interesting reports on the subject.

CAMP COOKING UTENSILS AND KITCHEN EQUIPMENT

The following list is intended as a check list for assembling camp cooking gear. Needless to say, no one camper will want to tote along the entire suggested outfit. Overlooking items is easy as the exciting day of departure approaches. The list is aimed solely at eliminating any oversights!

measuring cup
measuring spoons
polyethylene jars with lids
metal nesting mixing bowls
  or "dish-ups"
grater
mixing spoon
bottle opener
bread knife
paring knife
fillet knife
butcher knife
steak knives
biscuit cutter
pie plates
wire strainer
salt and pepper shakers
canister set
colander
saucepan
double boiler
percolator
drip coffee pot
guide's pot
tea pail
cook kit, nesting
polyethylene fruit-juice
  pitcher
wire meat broiler
square cast-iron skillet
round cast-iron skillet
steel fry pan
cast-iron griddle
toaster
Coleman oven
reflector oven

can opener
cake turner or spatula
muffin pan
gem tray
cake pan
cooky sheet
egg beater
wire whisk
French fryer
bread or pastry board
water bucket
pot lifters
asbestos glove
pot holders
corn popper
rubber plate scraper
aluminum foil
flour sifter
egg box
folding water bottle
cheese slicer
egg slicer
food tongs
dipper
ladle
ice pick
fish scaler
camp-stove lighter
soup bowls
butter dish
paper towels
paper napkins
vacuum bottle
tablecloth
tablecloth clips

Dutch oven
food chopper
meat grinder
barbecue set
water cooler
dish pan
dish towels
sponge
dish mop
rubber plate scraper
scouring pads
pressure cooker
garbage bags
bread box
matches
night light
first aid kit

disposable aluminum plates
rubber gloves
small carving board
knife sharpener
shredder
drinking cups
paper cups
paper plates
cereal bowls
paper cup dispenser
cup hooks
detergent
skewers
plastic food wrapper
toothpicks
dinner bell
small fire extinguisher

STAPLES

A—1 sauce
allspice

baking powder
baking soda
barbecue sauce
barley
basil
bay leaf
biscuit mix
bouillon cubes

candy
catsup
celery salt
cereals, dry
cheese, grated
chervil
chile powder
chives

chocolate, unsweetened
chopped nuts
cinnamon
citrus crystals
cloves
cocoa
coconut, shredded
coffee
cooking oil
corn meal
cornstarch
corn syrup
cream of tartar
cream, powdered
curry powder

extracts
    almond
    lemon
    maple

orange
vanilla

figs
flour
french dressing
fruit juice, powered

garlic
garlic powder
ginger
grapefruit juice crystals
gravy mixes
grits, quick

hominy grits
honey

jams
jellies

lemonade, instant
lemon extract
lemon juice, concentrated

macaroni
mace
maple syrup
marjoram
marmalade
marshmallow fluff
marshmallows
mayonnaise
meat tenderizer
milk, evaporated
  instant nonfat
  instant chocolate
mint
mixes
  biscuit
  cake
  gravy

muffin
pancake
pie crust
sauce
syrup
molasses
mustard, dry
  prepared

noodles
nutmeg
nuts, chopped

oats, rolled
olive oil
onion flakes
onion salt
orange juice mix,
  dehydrated
oregano

pancake mix
paprika
parsley flakes
pastry mixes
peanut butter
pepper
pineapple juice crystals
popcorn
poultry seasoning

raisins
rice, instant
rosemary
russian dressing

saccharin
sage
salad dressing
salad oil
salt

shortening
soy sauce
sugar, brown
  confectioners
  granulated

tapioca, quick
tarragon

tea, bags
  bulk
thyme

vanilla extract
vinegar

worcestershire sauce

yeast

STAND-BYS

apple butter
apples, fresh
apple juice
applesauce
apricots, dried
asparagus, canned

bacon
beans, canned, baked, dried
beef, canned, roast
  chipped
beets, canned
blackberries, fresh
  canned
broccoli
brown bread, canned
brussels sprouts
butter

cabbage
Canadian bacon
carrots, fresh
  canned
cauliflower
cheese
cheese spreads
cherries, fresh
  canned
chicken à la king, canned
  chow mein, canned

  " " dinner
  fricassee, canned
  spread
  stew, canned
chile con carne, canned
chop suey, canned
  " " dinner
clam chowder, canned
cookies
corn, cream style, canned
  whole kernel, canned
  chowder, canned
  niblets
  on-the-cob, fresh
corned beef, canned
crab meat, canned
crackers
cranberry sauce, canned

dates, pitted
dehydrated foods
deviled ham, canned

egg-noodle-chicken dinner
eggplant
eggs, fresh

fish, smoked
  dried
frankfurters, canned

freeze-dried foods
fruit, canned
   dried
   fresh
fruit juice mix, dehydrated

grapefruit, fresh
   juice, canned
grapejuice, canned
green beans, canned

ham, canned
   smoked
hash, canned, corned beef
   canned, roast beef
horticultural beans, canned

lard
lemons, fresh
lima beans, canned
lobster meat, canned
luncheon meat, canned

macaroni and cheese,
   canned
   dehydrated dinners
mandarin oranges, canned
Mex-i-Corn
mushrooms, canned
   fresh

oleomargarine
olives
onions, whole fresh
orange juice, canned
oranges, fresh
oysters, canned

peaches, canned
   fresh
pears, canned

fresh
peas, canned
peppers, green
   red
pickles
pineapple, canned
   juice
pizza pie mix
plums
potatoes, fresh
   canned
   instant
   sticks
   chips
prepared dinners
prunes
pudding mixes
   whole, canned
pumpkin, canned
punch, canned, fruit

raspberries, canned
relishes
rhubarb
rice
   dehydrated dinners
roast beef, canned
roast beef gravy, canned

salami
salmon, canned
salt pork
sardines, canned
sauerkraut, canned
sausage, summer
shrimp, canned
Sloppy Joes, canned
soft drinks
soups, canned
   dried
spaghetti, canned

Soups and Chowders

Vegetables

New TOWER Books
of Exceptional Interest

T-095-9 TIME IS SHORT AND THE WATER RISES   95¢
—John Walsh, with Robert Gannon
Vivid, true-life account of the struggle to
save 10,000 doomed animals from a flooded
South American rain forest. Recommended
by the World Wildlife Fund.

T-075-9 I WAS THE NUREMBERG JAILER   15¢
—Colonel Burton C. Andrus
First-hand story of the Nazis at Nuremberg
by the man who was their jailer. All the facts
in vivid detail.

**T-125-7 COMPACT HISTORY OF THE INDIAN
WARS**—John Tebbel $1.25
Fascinating account of the Indian Wars that
raged in America for 300 years.

T-095-7 FAMILY CAMPERS' COOKBOOK   95¢
—Bill Riviere
Cookbook for the whole family on vacation.
Dozens of recipes, menus, equipment hints,
and the latest information on setting up
camp.

T-095-5 KEY TO NEEDLEPOINT   95¢
—Jack Heist
First paperback guide to America's fastest-
growing pastime. Complete instructions on
materials, equipment, stitches, old and new
designs.

T-075-11 THE AMAZING HYPNO-DIET   75¢
—Dorothy Sara
Practical guide to losing weight through hyp-
notism, self-suggestion, and the powers of the
unconscious.

T-075-1 GAMES WOMEN PLAY   75¢
—David Lynne
Fascinating study of the games and gambits
of women everywhere. How a man can turn
the trick and come out on top.

T-075-5 ESP AND PSYCHIC POWER   75¢
—Steven Tyler
Authoritative guide to ESP, witchcraft, the
occult; case histories of famous psychic
prophets.

New TOWER Books
of Exceptional Interest

AROUND THE KITCHEN LIKE MAGIC

Jean Laird

Tested tips to help save dollars, time, wear and tear by the popular columnist of "Women's Work" and "Around the House With Jean." Shows how to make life easier around the kitchen with time-savers, health hints, and beauty tips. Great for everyone from housewives to bachelors.

Tower   T-095-8   95¢

Please allow 3 weeks for filling orders.

Please allow 3 weeks for filling orders.